Scott Foresman

Reading

Grade 3

Leveled Reader Resource Guide

Scott Foresman

Editorial Offices: Glenview, Illinois • New York, New York
Sales Offices: Reading, Massachusetts • Duluth, Georgia • Glenview, Illinois
Carrollton, Texas • Menlo Park, California

Editorial Offices
Glenview, Illinois • New York, New York

Sales Offices
Reading, Massachusetts • Duluth, Georgia • Glenview, Illinois
Carrollton, Texas • Menlo Park, California

ISBN 0-673-59680-X

3 4 5 6 7 8 9 10-PO-06 05 04 03 02 01 00

Table of Contents

Unit 4　From Past to Present

Unit 5　Are We There Yet?

Unit 6　Imagination.kids

Introduction

The goal of *Scott Foresman Reading* is to help students not only become better readers in today's classroom, but also to build a love of reading that lasts a lifetime. Students who are having difficulty reading at grade level or reading fluently often develop negative attitudes about reading and themselves. Providing students with reading materials they can and want to read is the first step toward developing fluent readers. The Leveled Readers are a series of high interest, accessible materials that were developed to help students experience the joy of successful and meaningful reading. The Leveled Reader Resource Guide contains easy-to-use instructional plans, blackline masters, the Scott Foresman Leveling System, and assessment forms that will help you select Leveled Readers appropriate for students' abilities; instruct and support students before, during, and after reading; and assess their performance level.

About the Leveled Readers

There are 360 Leveled Readers in the *Scott Foresman Reading* program that are written one to one and a half grades below grade level. Set A is Easy. Set B is Easy/Average. For each Student Edition selection, there is a corresponding Set A Leveled Reader and a Set B Leveled Reader. Each one focuses on the same target comprehension skill, tested selection vocabulary, and theme as the Student Edition selection. The Leveled Readers increase in difficulty within a grade and from grade to grade. As students' reading abilities develop, they can begin reading texts with longer and more complex sentences, more pages, fewer illustrations, and more challenging concepts.

Grade	Number of Pages Per Leveled Reader
Grades 1–2	8–16 pages
Grades 3–4	16 pages
Grades 5–6	16–24 pages

See the Scott Foresman Leveling System on pages 154–155 for more information about how the Readers are leveled and to help you select Readers that match students' reading abilities. (There are also Set C/Challenge Leveled Readers, which provide literature and activities for students reading at or above grade level. Each Set C Leveled Reader is linked thematically to a unit in the Student Edition and gives students additional opportunities to expand target comprehension, vocabulary, and critical thinking skills. Instructional plans for Set C Leveled Readers can be found in a separate Resource Guide.)

Great care and attention were given to create Leveled Readers that are age appropriate and appealing to students for each grade level. The Leveled Readers provide students with a good mix of fiction and nonfiction texts in a variety of genres, such as fantasy, folk tale, realistic story, historical fiction, narrative nonfiction, biography, and how-to books. Many of the Leveled Readers for Grades 1–3 use predictable patterns of rhyme, rhythm, and sentence repetition to facilitate reading fluency. They include art on every page to ensure a good match between picture and text and to maximize comprehension. In all grades, there is a lively blend of humor, surprise, and novelty—characteristics that are very attractive to readers in Grades 1–6.

Using Leveled Readers

The Leveled Readers can be used to meet the diverse needs of your classroom in a variety of ways:

- as a means of developing fluency and reading skills and strategies for all students,

- as a substitute for the corresponding Student Edition selection for students who are reading below grade level,

- as a reinforcement of the corresponding Student Edition themes, tested selection vocabulary, and target comprehension skills for students reading at or below level,

- as a choice in Guided Reading groups,

- as a choice for self-selected reading,

- as a choice for shared reading,

- as a choice for a read aloud,

- as a choice for choral reading or to be performed as Readers Theater,

- as a choice for take-home reading,

- as a choice to be used in conjunction with the Instructional Routine Cards,

- as a text for assessment of oral reading and other reading skills and strategies.

Guided Reading

The instructional plans in the Leveled Reader Resource Guide were developed to be compatible with a guided-reading approach. This approach can be used with small groups of students who are reading at a similar reading level. Use the following routine to guide children before, during, and after reading.

- Select and introduce an appropriate Leveled Reader to the group.

- Have each student read (softly or silently), while you listen, assess, and provide support as needed.

- After reading, reinforce reading skills and strategies, assess comprehension, and help develop fluency by having students reread the text.

The goal in the guided-reading approach is to have students read independently, silently, and, above all, read for meaning.

Managing the Classroom

When you are using the Leveled Readers with individual students or in small groups, you will need to keep the other students engaged in independent and meaningful learning tasks. Establish different work stations around the classroom where students can be working on different tasks simultaneously. Display a work board that indicates the work stations and lists which students should be at each work station. Explain what task or tasks are to be done at each station and give an estimate of how long students should work there. Alert students when they should rotate to new stations and change their station assignments on the work board. Develop a classroom routine regarding the work stations and the rotation among these work stations so students can read and work more independently.

Work stations you can create are:

- Listening Work Station

- Phonics Work Station

- Technology Work Station

- Writing and Language Work Station

- Independent Reading Work Station

- Cross-Curricular Work Station

Using the Leveled Reader Resource Guide

Each Leveled Reader has its own instructional plan in the Leveled Reader Resource Guide, but all plans follow similar before, during, and after reading routines.

At a Glance

1 Links to the Student Edition   Each Leveled Reader is linked to a Student Edition selection and focuses on the same target comprehension skill, tested selection vocabulary (the group of tested words is divided between the A and B Leveled Readers), and unit theme.

Before Reading

2 Motivating the Reader   Create interest in the Leveled Reader by building background and connecting to what students already know. Suggestions are given for using pictures, videotapes, classroom discussion, graphic organizers, writing, art activities, or simple science experiments.

3 Preview and Predict   Preview the Leveled Reader by having students read the title and scan the cover, text, and illustrations. Have students make predictions about what happens in the story or what information they will find in the book. Then suggest a purpose for reading or have them set their own. Point out selection vocabulary and any unfamiliar words or expressions that might be important to understanding the book.

During Reading

4 Guiding Comprehension   Have students read the Leveled Reader, either softly or silently, to a specific point in the book or the entire book. Then use the questions provided as needed to support and assess students' comprehension.

5 Ongoing Assessment   Listen and watch for students to use effective reading strategies as they read. Use the If/Then statements provided to help students develop better reading strategies and build self-awareness and confidence about the good reading strategies they do use. Make notes about students' reading performance, using the Observation Checklist on page 156, Taking a Running Record on page 157, or the Anecdotal Record on page 158.

6 Model Your Thinking   If students have difficulty with the target comprehension skill, then use the Think Aloud model provided to help students understand what the skill is, why it is a useful skill, and how this skill can be used to understand the Leveled Reader better.

After Reading

7 Revisiting the Text   Students will better comprehend the text and develop fluency by rereading the Leveled Reader independently, with a partner, or in a small group. Activity suggestions are given to help students organize their thinking, respond to what they've read, and demonstrate their understanding of the Leveled Reader and the target comprehension skill.

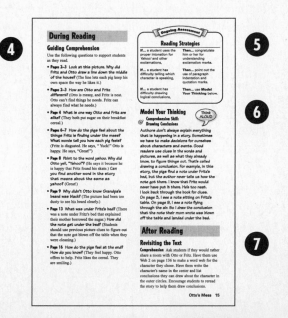

Using the Blackline Masters

Blackline masters can be found on pages 130–153. These blackline masters are a set of twenty-four graphic organizers that can be copied onto plastic transparency sheets and used on a overhead projector or copied onto paper for students to use as worksheets. Suggestions are given in the instructional plans for ways to customize and use these graphic organizers.

Assessing Performance

If/Then statements are provided in each instructional plan to help you assess and assist students as they read the Leveled Reader. Use the assessment forms that begin on page 156 to make notes about students' reading skills, strategies, and behaviors as they read.

- **Observation Checklist** (p. 156) Allows you to note the regularity with which students demonstrate their understanding and use of reading skills and strategies.

- **Taking a Running Record** (p. 157) Tells how to take a running record so you can calculate a student's reading accuracy and reading rate. (See also the sample Running Record on the next page.)

- **Anecdotal Record** (p. 158) Allows you record anecdotal examples of students' behaviors and attitudes regarding reading, such as noting a student who showed a particular interest in a specific topic or type of response activity or a student who may daydream during free reading because he or she found the self-selected book too challenging.

- **Student Self-Assessment** (p. 159) Helps students identify their own areas of strength and areas where they need further work. It encourages them to list steps they can take to become better readers and to set goals that they can then work to accomplish. Have students share their self-assessment notes with their families and work with them to practice their reading skills and strategies at home.

- **Progress Report** (p. 160) Allows you to track a student's book-reading progress over a period of time by noting the level at which a student reads and their accuracy rate at that level. Reading the chart from left to right gives you a visual model of how quickly a student is making the transition from one level to the next. Share these reports with parents or guardians to help them see how their child's reading is progressing.

Use these assessment forms along with the Scott Foresman Leveling System on pages 154–155 to help you decide whether a student can make the transition to reading materials at the next, more challenging level (student consistently reads at an independent level with an accuracy rate of 98% or better), needs further practice and guided instruction with materials at the same level (student reads at an instructional level with an accuracy rate between 91–97%), or needs targeted instruction and intervention with materials developed for a lower level (student reads at a frustrational level with an accuracy rate below 90%). See the Assessment Handbook for further ideas and forms to help you assess students.

Taking a Running Record

The sample on the next page shows the miscues a student made while reading aloud. See page 144 for more information on taking a running record and assessing the results. Use the notations in the sample to identify the kinds of miscues the student makes while reading. Count the number of errors and subtract them from the total number of words to find the number of words the student read correctly. Divide the number of words read correctly by the total number of words to find the student's accuracy rate. If the student makes the same error more than once, such as mispronouncing *exactly* twice, count it as one error. If possible, tape-record the student reading so you can check your running record. Calculate the reading rate by dividing the total number of words by the number of seconds the student took to read the text. Multiply by sixty to find how many words per minute the student can read. End by having the student summarize the text, so you can assess his or her comprehension of it.

Running Record Sample

Fritz and Otto drew a line down the

middle of their cozy house. Fritz lived

side

on the right. Otto lived on the ~~left~~. Fritz

kept his things neat. Otto's things were

very

not ~~exactly~~ neat.

/klen/

Fritz kept his things clean. Otto's

things were not exactly clean. Fritz

could always find what he needed. Otto

could never find what he needed.

But Fritz and Otto did one thing the

same. They both made their breakfast

H   *sc*

<u>cereal</u> sweet with sugar. That was how

their mom always fixed it. So Fritz and

Otto shared the sugar jar.

—From *Otto's Mess,*
Leveled Reader 62A,
Grade 3

Total Number of Words: _93_

Number of Errors: _5_

Accuracy Percentage Score: _95%_

Reading Time: _70 sec_

Reading Rate: _80 wpm_

Miscues

Omission The student omits words or word parts.

Insertion The student inserts words or parts of words that are not in the text.

Substitution The student substitutes words or parts of words for the words in the text.

Mispronunciation/Misreading The student pronounces or reads a word incorrectly.

Hesitation The student hesitates over a word and the teacher provides the word. Wait several seconds before telling the child what the word is.

Self-correction The student reads a word incorrectly but then corrects the error. Do not count self-corrections as actual errors. However, noting self-corrections will help you identify words the student finds difficult.

$$\frac{93-5}{93} = \frac{88}{93} = .946 = 95\%$$

$$\frac{93}{70} \times 60 = 79.7 = 80 \text{ words per minute}$$

61A
The Wild West

by Myka-Lynne Sokoloff
Leveled Reader 61A
Genre: Humorous Story
Level: Easy

Summary

A young girl and her family visit a dude ranch. The girl enjoys imagining how things were in the "Wild West" and has many adventures. Some are exciting, and some are embarrassing, but all are lots of fun.

At a Glance

Links to the Student Edition

⌖ **Comprehension Skill:** Sequence

Selection Vocabulary: *cowboys, summer, west, imagination*

Program Theme: Myself and Others
Unit Theme: Finding My Place

When we learn about how others live, we learn things about ourselves as well.

Before Reading

Motivating the Reader
Build Background About Imagination

Name a place where it is unlikely that students have ever visited. Or name a time period and have students think about their town at that time. Ask students to imagine what the place might look like, what people's homes might look like, and what people might wear. Then ask students to draw a picture of what they imagine. Discuss their pictures, and point out that each of them have imagined different things. If possible, show students realistic pictures of the area or time period, and have them compare these pictures to their own drawings.

Preview and Predict

Have students scan the cover, text and illustrations to get an idea of what the book is about. Ask them to predict whether the story will be funny or serious and tell why they made the prediction they did. Use Web 1 on page 132 and write *Wild West* in the center of the web. Record students' ideas about what they think the "Wild West" is like. Encourage students to make predictions about what the book's characters will find in the Wild West.

Point out selection vocabulary and any unfamiliar words, such as *bandanna, cactus,* and *bronco,* that might be important to understanding the book.

During Reading

Guiding Comprehension

Use the following questions to support students as they read.

- **Pages 2–3** Where is the family going? (on a trip out west) **What is the girl imagining?** (She is imagining she and her family are traveling out west in a covered wagon.)

- **Pages 2–3** How does the illustrator show what the girl is imagining? (Students should point out the thought balloons in the picture. If necessary, explain that thought balloons, like the one shown here, are used to show what people are thinking or imagining. See also pages 12 and 16.)

- **Page 5** What cowboy clothes does the girl and family get? Point to these items in the picture. (They get boots, hats, and bandannas.)

- **Page 6** What do the sentences "I went one way. My new boots went the other way." mean? Use the picture to help you. (Her feet twisted around when she moved forward.)

- **Pages 6–7** Why did the girl fall into the tub? (She was not used to wearing big boots, so she tripped when she ran.)

- **Page 8** Why did the girl think they might eat rattlesnake for dinner? (She thought eating habits might be very different in the wild west.)

- **Pages 9–11** What happened after the cookout? (They told stories, the family slept in a tent, and the girl got nervous remembering the scary stories she heard.)

- **Page 11** Did a big cactus really come after the girl? (No, it was just the cactus's shadow that frightened the girl.)

- **Pages 12–13** What did the girl do after playing tag? (She and her family all said good-by to their new friends, and the girl promised to write.)

Ongoing Assessment

Reading Strategies

If... a student has trouble with the word *scary* on page 9,	**Then...** help the student use the base word *scare* to understand *scary*.
If... students have difficulty identifying the order of events or in summarizing what they've read,	**Then...** encourage them to re-read a specific passage more slowly and look for clue words like *next* or *then*.
If... a student has difficulty following the sequence of events,	**Then...** use **Model Your Thinking** below.

Model Your Thinking

🎯 **Comprehension Skill: Sequence**

Sequence means the order in which things happen. Good readers keep track of the sequence of events in a story because it helps them make sense of the story and remember the important events. Clue words, such as *first*, *next*, or *finally*, can help you identify and remember the order of events. For instance, on page 8, the girl tells us that "First we had a cookout." Then, on page 9 we find the sentence "Next, we told stories until dark." These clue words tell us that the story telling happened after the *cookout*. Sometimes, though, there are no clue words, and we have to figure out the order of events.

After Reading

Revisiting the Text

Comprehension Ask the students to pretend to be the girl in the story. Challenge them to write a diary entry about their vacation. First have students review the book and use the Plot/Story Sequence organizer on page 137 to list events. The middle box will have many entries, so you may wish to model how to do this part. Students can use their organizers to help them write their diary entries.

61B
Mr. Kidd

by Robert R. O'Brien
Leveled Reader 61B
Genre: Fantasy
Level: Easy/Average

Summary

Aunt Babs, an inventor, brings home a robot named Mr. Kidd. At first her nephew is delighted with the new companion. However when the robot begins to copy the actions it sees on TV, things rapidly get out of hand. Eventually, Aunt Babs takes Mr. Kidd away. At the end, the nephew wonders if things will now return to normal. Readers are left wondering too as they discover that the nephew's new companion is also a robot.

At a Glance

Links to the Student Edition

☞ **Comprehension Skill:** Sequence

Selection Vocabulary: *visit, summer, vacation*

Program Theme: Myself and Others
Unit Theme: Finding My Place

Robots can sometimes act like humans, but when their programming gets messed up, we see how different they really are.

Before Reading

Motivating the Reader
Build Background About Robots

Have volunteers work in pairs. One partner pretends to be a robot that acts out the commands of its human inventor. Remind the "humans" that their commands must be simple and clear. Remind the "robots" that they can do only what is commanded and must continue this action until commanded to stop. After a few pairs have performed, you may wish to use Web 1 on page 132 to generate ideas about robots. Write the word *robot* in the web's center and have students list details or draw pictures about the subject.

Preview and Predict

Have students scan the cover, text, and the illustrations. Then have them use the Story Prediction organizer on page 130. Ask students to write the title of the book and have them make a prediction about what problem the book might show. Encourage students to read to find out how the problems in the book are solved. Students can complete the organizer once they are done reading the book.

Point out selection vocabulary and any unfamiliar words, such as *invention, squirted,* or *terrified,* that might be important to understanding the book.

During Reading

Guiding Comprehension

Use the following questions to support students as they read.

- **Pages 2–3** *What do the pictures on these pages show?* (It shows one of Aunt Babs' inventions that doesn't work well.)

- **Page 5** *What gets squirted all over Mr. Kidd? What other words mean the same as squirted?* (a can of juice; spilled, splashed)

- **Page 5** *What did the spilled juice do to the robot?* (It made it act in funny ways.)

- **Page 5** *What was the first thing that happened after the juice was spilled on Mr. Kidd?* (He sang along with the TV character.)

- **Page 6** *What did the robot try to do next?* (It tried to fly.) Repeat this question for other incidents in the story.

- **Page 7** *Why were the fish terrified?* (Mr. Kidd was acting like a shark. He put his head in the fish tank.)

- **Pages 7–11** *What happens each time the boy changes the TV channel?* (The robot imitates what it sees on the TV channel.)

- **Page 11** *What does Mr. Kidd do with the can opener? Look at the radio, toaster, table, and Mr. Kidd's head.* (Mr. Kidd used the can opener on the radio, toaster, and his head.)

- **Page 13** *Why did the boy turn the TV off?* (He turned the TV off so the robot wouldn't try to imitate what it saw on the TV.)

- **Page 16–17** *Do you think things will get back to normal? Why or why not?* (No. The woman playing checkers looks like a real person, but she is a robot, so things will probably not be normal.)

Ongoing Assessment

Reading Strategies

If... a student hesitates over the word *squirted*,	**Then...** ask the student to look at the picture and use the context and illustration to interpret the text.
If... a student cannot understand what causes Mr. Kidd's behavior to change,	**Then...** encourage the student to compare images on the TV set with Mr. Kidd's actions.
If... a student has difficulty following the sequence of events,	**Then...** use **Model Your Thinking** below.

Model Your Thinking

 Comprehension Skill: Sequence

The story in this book is told in a certain sequence, or order. As I read, I try to imagine what is happening, and how the events may be related to each other. I look for clue words such as *first, next,* and *finally,* to figure out the order in which things happen. If I can figure out the sequence, or the order of events, I will understand a story better. For instance, after the juice is spilled, the robot starts singing along with the TV character. Then, when Captain Crispy starts flying, Mr. Kidd also tries to fly. Knowing that Mr. Kidd started acting strange after the juice got squirted on him helps me understand the book better.

After Reading

Revisiting the Text

Comprehension Have pairs reread the book and use the Story Elements organizer on page 144 to describe story events in the order they happen. Pairs can then use their organizers to draw comic strips to retell the story. They can cut their strips into individual panels and exchange them with other pairs. Students can arrange one another's strips in correct order.

62A

Otto's Mess

by Sydnie Meltzer Kleinhenz
Leveled Reader 62A
Genre: Animal Fantasy
Level: Easy

Summary

When the sugar jar is missing, Fritz, a very neat pig, decides it's time to clean up his brother Otto's messy half of the house. Later, they find a note that reveals that their mom has borrowed the sugar. The house is clean, but Fritz is still frustrated, until Otto makes him a messy—but delicious!—substitute breakfast.

At a Glance

Links to the Student Edition

⌖ **Comprehension Skill:** Drawing Conclusions

Selection Vocabulary: *breakfast, cozy, gobbled, hungry*

Program Theme: Myself and Others
Unit Theme: Finding My Place

Even brothers who are complete opposites can learn from one another.

Before Reading

Motivating the Reader
Build Background About the Concept of Sharing

Ask for two volunteers to role-play. Place two chairs and other props side by side at the front of the room. Instruct one player to be a very messy character and the other to be a very neat character as they role-play the difficulties the two characters have sharing a room. Encourage students to discuss the characters' problem and suggest possible solutions. Ask students to think about the challenges of sharing as they read the book.

Preview and Predict

Have students scan the cover, text, and illustrations to get an idea of what the book is about. Prepare students to read by drawing their attention to the book's cover, opening it to show the front and back. Ask them to read the title and predict which character in the illustration is Otto. Encourage students to make predictions about the characters' personalities and what might happen in the book.

Point out selection vocabulary and any unfamiliar words, such as *sugar* and *cereal,* that might be important to understanding the book.

During Reading

Guiding Comprehension

Use the following questions to support students as they read.

- **Pages 2–3** **Look at this picture. Why did Fritz and Otto draw a line down the middle of the house?** (The line lets each pig keep his own space the way he likes it.)

- **Pages 2–3** **How are Otto and Fritz different?** (Otto is messy, and Fritz is neat. Otto can't find things he needs. Fritz can always find what he needs.)

- **Page 4** **What is one way Otto and Fritz are alike?** (They both put sugar on their breakfast cereal.)

- **Pages 6–7** **How do the pigs feel about the things Fritz is finding under the mess? What words tell you how each pig feels?** (Fritz is disgusted. He says, " Yuck!" Otto is happy. He says, "Great!")

- **Page 8** **Point to the word yahoo. Why did Otto yell, "Yahoo!"?** (He says it because he is happy that Fritz found his skate.) **Can you find another word in the story that means about the same as yahoo?** (Great!)

- **Page 9** **Why didn't Otto know Grandpa's beard was black?** (The picture had been too dusty to see his beard clearly.)

- **Page 13** **What was under Fritz's bed?** (There was a note under Fritz's bed that explained their mother borrowed the sugar.) **How did the note get under the bed?** (Students should use previous picture clues to figure out that the note got blown off the table when they were cleaning.)

- **Page 16** **How do the pigs feel at the end? How do you know?** (They feel happy. Otto offers to help. Fritz likes the cereal. They are smiling.)

Ongoing Assessment

Reading Strategies

If... a student uses the proper intonation for *Yahoo!* and other exclamations,	**Then...** congratulate him or her for understanding exclamation marks.
If... a student has difficulty telling which character is speaking,	**Then...** point out the use of paragraph indentation and quotation marks.
If... a student has difficulty drawing logical conclusions,	**Then...** use **Model Your Thinking** below.

Model Your Thinking

 **Comprehension Skill: Drawing Conclusions**

 Think **ALOUD**

Authors don't always explain everything that is happening in a story. Sometimes we have to make decisions for ourselves about characters and events. Good readers use clues in the words and pictures, as well as what they already know, to figure things out. That's called drawing a conclusion. For example, in this story, the pigs find a note under Fritz's bed, but the author never tells us how the note got there. I know that Fritz would never have put it there. He's too neat. I look back through the book for clues. On page 3, I see a note sitting on Fritz's table. On page 9, I see a note flying through the air. So I draw the conclusion that the note their mom wrote was blown off the table and landed under the bed.

After Reading

Revisiting the Text

Comprehension Ask students if they would rather share a room with Otto or Fritz. Have them use Web 2 on page 133 to make a word web for the character they chose. Have them write the character's name in the center and list conclusions they can draw about the character in the outer circles. Encourage students to reread the story to help them draw conclusions.

62B

If You Were a Teacher

by Fay Robinson
Leveled Reader 62B
Genre: Narrative Nonfiction
Level: Easy/Average

Summary

Readers see a typical day in the life of an elementary teacher. The book gives a realistic idea of the many responsibilities a teacher has and the different kinds of things that a teacher does as a regular part of his or her job.

At a Glance

Links to the Student Edition

◔ **Comprehension Skill:** Drawing Conclusions

Selection Vocabulary: *comfortable, forest, promise*

Program Theme: Myself and Others
Unit Theme: Finding My Place

A good way to learn about others is to imagine what it would be like to be them, at least for a day.

Before Reading

Motivating the Reader
Build Background About a Teacher's Job

Ask volunteers to act as the class teacher to lead a variety of familiar class routines. Encourage students to ask questions of the "teacher." Afterward, point out some of the many things a teacher must know in order to perform the specific tasks that a teacher does each day. As students prepare to read the book, encourage them to think about what they would do if they were a teacher for a day.

Preview and Predict

Have students scan the cover, text and illustrations to get an idea of what the book is about. Then have students use the K-W-L Chart on page 135. Have them write in the first column what they know about a teacher's job. In the next column have them write questions about what they would like to know about being a teacher. When students have finished reading the book, they can complete the last column by listing the new information they have learned. Encourage students to use what they know about teachers to make predictions about what tasks the teacher will do in this book.

Point out selection vocabulary and any unfamiliar words such as *college, flick,* and *model,* that might be important to understanding the book.

During Reading

Guiding Comprehension

Use the following questions to support students as they read.

- **Page 2** Why must the teacher not be late for school? (The teacher needs to be in the classroom before the students arrive.)

- **Page 3** Look at the phrase "to set things up." What does this phrase mean? What things might a teacher need "to set up"? (The phrase means "to prepare things." The "things" might be all the items that the students and the teacher will need for that day's school work.)

- **Page 4** Look at the phrase "keep track of." What does this phrase mean? (It means "remembering or making notes about something.")

- **Page 6** What does the word *flick* mean as used in this sentence? Use the picture and the context to help you decide. (In this case, it means turning the lights on and off rapidly.)

- **Page 8** Where does a teacher learn to teach subjects, such as reading, writing, and math? (at college)

- **Page 10** Why are there two pictures of the teacher eating lunch on this page? (The pictures show the two places that a teacher might eat lunch.)

- **Page 11** Find a model on this page that a teacher might use to teach about bones. (Students should point to the dinosaur model.)

- **Page 12** What do you think the children are doing in the picture? (They are trying to put together the dinosaur bones.)

- **Page 16** Why might a teacher be tired at the end of the day? (A teacher has many things to do all day and stays later than the students.)

Reading Strategies

If... a student stumbles over the word *pears* on page 8,

Then... tell the student to look at the illustration, which will give a clue as to what the object is.

If... a student has difficulty drawing logical conclusions,

Then... use **Model Your Thinking** below.

Model Your Thinking

Comprehension Skill: Drawing Conclusions

Think ALOUD

A conclusion is a decision you reach after you think about the details or facts in what you have read. To draw conclusions, I use evidence from the story and what I know from my own experiences. For instance, on page 2, I see that the teacher is carrying a briefcase as she comes to school. On page 16, I see she is carrying the briefcase again as she goes home. Even though the author never says anything about the briefcase, I can draw the conclusion that she probably takes it home at night and brings it back in the morning. I also know that people usually carry papers in a briefcase, so I think that she probably carries her work from school to finish it at home.

After Reading

Revisiting the Text

Comprehension Have pairs reread the book together and complete the K-W-L Charts they started before they read the book. Have students use their charts to help them decide whether a teacher's job is easy or difficult. Have pairs write their conclusions and list reasons why a teacher's job is easy or difficult.

63A
Ready for the Rodeo

by Jack Rummel
Leveled Reader 63A
Genre: Narrative Nonfiction
Level: Easy

Summary

Tex lives with his family on a cattle ranch and dreams of being in a rodeo someday. He practices his cowboy skills and helps his dad with chores on the ranch. On a trip to the high corral, Tex succeeds in roping a calf. His father is pleased and assures Tex that someday he will be a fine rodeo cowboy.

At a Glance

Links to the Student Edition

☞ **Comprehension Skill:** Author's Purpose

Selection Vocabulary: *rodeo, practice, grandfather, prepare*

Program Theme: Myself and Others
Unit Theme: Finding My Place

We need to learn many skills and practice them if we wish to fulfill our dreams when we grow up.

Before Reading

Motivating the Reader
Build Background About Ranches

Show students pictures or a videotape of a real-life ranch. Ask students to name things you might see or do on a ranch. List students' ideas on the chalkboard. Invite volunteers to act out a task a ranch hand might do, such as riding a horse or fixing a fence. As students prepare to read the book, encourage them to think about what skills a ranch hand needs to perform these tasks.

Preview and Predict

Have students scan the cover, text, and illustrations. Encourage them to use picture clues and familiar words to make a prediction of what the book is about and whether it will show realistic or make-believe events. Students can set their own purpose for reading, such as trying to find out what kinds of skills are needed to be a ranch hand or a rodeo cowboy/cowgirl.

Point out selection vocabulary and any unfamiliar words such as *chores, shoe, mend, clucked,* and *spurred,* that might be important to understanding the book.

During Reading

Guiding Comprehension

Use the following questions to support students as they read.

- **Page 2** *Where does Tex live?* (Tex lives on a ranch in New Mexico.)

- **Page 4** *What is another word that means almost the same as chores?* (jobs or tasks) *What chores do Tex and his father do?* (They shoe horses, fix fences, and feed the cattle.)

- **Page 4** *What does the word tradition mean in this book? Use context clues to help you.* (It means "something passed down" from one family member to another, such as from father to son.)

- **Page 5** *Why is Tex's horse called a paint?* (The horse has splashes of white on brown that look like patches of paint.)

- **Pages 6–7** *Why would roping be useful on a cattle ranch?* (Cowboys use ropes to capture cows.)

- **Page 8** *What does this page tell you about rodeos?* (Cowboys ride bulls in front of an audience, and the best ones are given prizes. The bulls are big and scary.)

- **Page 10** *What do you think a pack horse is used for? Use the context and the illustrations to help you.* (A pack horse is used to carry supplies.)

- **Page 11** *What does the expression "They made it!" mean in this book.* (The horse made a difficult jump. He and Tex landed safely on the other side.)

- **Pages 14–15** *What steps does Tex do to rope a calf?* (He grabs his rope, twirls it, and tosses it at a running calf's back feet. He pulls the rope together to catch and stop the calf.)

- **Page 16** *Why do you think the author wrote this book?* (to tell an interesting story, to explain about life on a ranch and rodeos)

Reading Strategies

If... a student uses the proper intonation for the exclamations on pages 8, 11, and 16,	**Then...** praise the student for recognizing that exclamation marks are used to show strong feeling.
If... a student does not understand the use of *shoe* as a verb on page 4,	**Then...** have the student look at the picture and describe what Tex's father is doing.
If... a student has difficulty explaining why the author may have written the book,	**Then...** use **Model Your Thinking** below.

Model Your Thinking

 Comprehension Skill: Author's Purpose

Think ALOUD

An author's purpose is the reason or reasons why an author writes something. Authors may write to entertain readers, to express a mood or feeling, to convince you to think or act a certain way, or to explain something. As I read this book, I notice that it tells a lot about life on a ranch, such as what a paint is or what a corral is, so I think one reason the author wrote this book was to explain something. Thinking about the author's purpose helps me better understand the book.

After Reading

Revisiting the Text

Comprehension Have students use Web 1 on page 132. Have them write in the center *Life on a Ranch*. Students can then list facts they learned about ranches from reading the book. Then have students use their webs to write a sentence describing the author's purpose.

63B

Tad Lucas, Cowgirl

by Lilly Ernesto
Leveled Reader 63B
Genre: Biography
Level: Easy/Average

Summary

Tad Barnes Lucas could ride a horse from the time she was very little. When she was fourteen, she rode for the first time in a contest and won. Tad practiced trick riding and training horses. She won championships year after year and even started an all-girl rodeo. For many years she was the top cowgirl in the land.

At a Glance

Links to the Student Edition

Comprehension Skill: Author's Purpose

Selection Vocabulary: *favorite, rodeo, tourists, practice*

Program Theme: Myself and Others
Unit Theme: Finding My Place

A lot of practice and a love of one's work can lead to a rich and satisfying life.

Before Reading

Motivating the Reader
Build Background About Rodeos

If possible, show a videotape or photographs of a rodeo to give students an idea of what happens at a rodeo. If any students are familiar with these events, ask them to describe or act out what happens at a rodeo. For example, students can sit backwards on a chair and pretend it's a bucking bronco. Have students use the T-Chart on page 150 to list reasons why they would or would not want to be in a rodeo. As students prepare to read the book, encourage them to think about why the main character loves riding in rodeos.

Preview and Predict

Have students scan the cover, text, and illustrations. Encourage them to use picture clues and familiar words to predict what the book is about. Encourage students to decide whether the book tells about a real person's life or is a made-up story. Have them give reasons to support their decisions. Suggest students read to find out who Tad Lucas was and what she did.

Point out selection vocabulary and any unfamiliar words, such as *bucked, steer, reared,* and *spring* (verb), that might be important to understanding the book.

During Reading

Guiding Comprehension

Use the following questions to support students as they read.

- **Page 2** What talent did Tad have? (She could ride a horse at a very early age.)

- **Page 3** Read the words on this page. Then look at the picture. Which child in the picture is Tad? (Tad was the youngest child in the family. She is probably the infant being held by the person on horseback.)

- **Page 5** How did Tad get to school? (She rode her horse Black to school.)

- **Page 6** Why do the horses need to be trained? (Untrained horses try to throw riders off their backs.)

- **Page 9** What does the phrase "the crowd's favorite" mean? Use the picture to help you. (It means the people cheering liked Tad the most.)

- **Pages 10–11** What were the tricks that Tad learned to do through long and hard practice? Use the pictures to help you. (She learned to ride standing up, she sprang or jumped over a galloping horse, and she slid under a horse's belly as it ran at top speed.)

- **Page 13** How do you know Tad was a great trick rider? (She won the trick riding championship many times.)

- **Page 14** How soon after Tad broke her arm was she riding again? (She was able to ride again one year later.)

- **Page 16** What words would you use to describe Tad Lucas? (Answers will vary.)

- **Page 16** Why do you think the author wrote this book? (to tell about Tad Lucas's life)

Ongoing Assessment

Reading Strategies

If... a student does not understand Tad's trick riding stunts,	**Then...** have the student look carefully at the pictures one by one as he or she rereads the part of the text that names each stunt.
If... a student has difficulty connecting Tad Barnes with Tad Lucas,	**Then...** have the student reread page 14 and explain that women often change their last names when they get married.
If... a student has difficulty explaining why the author may have written the book,	**Then...** use **Model Your Thinking** below.

Model Your Thinking

 Comprehension Skill: Author's Purpose

Think ALOUD

When good readers think about the author's purpose, they ask themselves: "Why did the author write this book?" There are many reasons why people write. Some of the main reasons are: to inform, which means to tell us about something or someone; to persuade, which means to try to make us believe, or agree with, something; to entertain, which means to tell an interesting story; or to express strong feelings, as in writing a poem. Because this book has so many facts about Tad Barnes Lucas, I think the author wrote to inform—to tell us about someone very special.

After Reading

Revisiting the Text

Comprehension Have students review the text and write a sentence that describes the author's purpose. Then have students use the Time Line on page 143 to list interesting facts about Tad Lucas.

64A
Special Delivery

by Anne Phillips
Leveled Reader 64A
Genre: Realistic Story
Level: Easy

Summary

As Anna delivers the mail, she brings gifts of special cheer to the people on her route who are ill. However, one day Anna gets sick and cannot deliver the mail. Then her friends each bring her the same remedy that she gave to them when they were ill. A now healthy Anna delivers thank-you notes to all her friends.

At a Glance

Links to the Student Edition

☞ **Comprehension Skill:** Cause and Effect

Selection Vocabulary: *coughs, pretend, sheet, curious*

Program Theme: Myself and Others
Unit Theme: Finding My Place

A good friend or neighbor tries to help others in need.

Before Reading

Motivating the Reader
Build Background About the Concept of Helping Others

Engage students in a role-playing activity. Have volunteers play each of the following roles: a new child in class, a sick friend, and a child lost in a shopping mall. Have several other students approach the person who has a problem and show what he or she might do to help. After each scene, discuss the kinds of help that was offered. Invite the students to decide which offers were the most helpful. Ask them to discuss what kind of help they would want if they were in trouble.

Preview and Predict

Have students scan the cover, text, and illustrations to get an idea of what the book is about. Encourage them to use picture clues and familiar words to make predictions about who the main character is and what she does. Discuss the title, *Special Delivery*, and point out that the title can help them with their predictions.

Point out selection vocabulary and any unfamiliar words, such as *envelope, package, chicken pox,* and *delivered,* that might be important to understanding the book.

During Reading

Guiding Comprehension

Use the following questions to support students as they read.

- **Page 2** Who is Anna? What does she do? (Anna delivers mail.)

- **Page 3** Why was Mrs. Blue curious? (She was curious because Anna took a large envelope out of her bag.)

- **Page 4** Why did Mrs. Blue feel better? (She felt better because Anna delivered a get-well card.)

- **Page 6** What happened when Mr. Green ate the hot soup? (He felt better.)

- **Page 8** What makes Dan and Nan feel better? (Anna brought them a box full of games and toys.)

- **Page 9** What has happened in the book so far? (Anna has brought something special to each of her friends who is sick.)

- **Page 9** What does *delivered* mean? What other word would make sense in these sentences? (brought)

- **Pages 10–11** What two things happened because Anna did not deliver the mail? (Her friends were worried. They all went to Anna's house.)

- **Page 12** What do you think is the matter with Anna? Why do you think so? (Her nose and eyes are red and she sneezes and coughs, so she probably has a cold.)

- **Page 13** What do you think the people might have in their bags? (Answers will vary, but students should recognize that Anna's friends are probably bringing things to help Anna feel better.)

- **Page 16** Why did Anna deliver thank-you cards? (She wanted to thank her friends who brought her gifts.)

Reading Strategies

If... a student does not know what chicken pox is,	**Then...** have the student reread pages 7–8 and examine the children's faces in the illustration.
If... a student reads the declarative and exclamatory sentences with the same inflection,	**Then...** call the student's attention to the different end punctuation marks and model the appropriate inflection.
If... a student cannot recognize cause-and-effect relationships,	**Then...** use **Model Your Thinking** below.

Model Your Thinking

 Comprehension Skill: Cause and Effect

 Think ALOUD

A cause is why something happens. An effect is what happens. Sometimes clue words such as *if, then, because,* and *so* signal causes and effects. To find the cause of something, I ask myself: Why did it happen? To find the effect, I ask: What happened? For example, on page 6, I look at the picture of Mr. Green and ask myself: What happened to Mr. Green? I read to find out that Mr. Green feels better. Then I ask: Why does he feel better? He feels better because he ate the soup Anna brought.

After Reading

Revisiting the Text

Comprehension Have students use the Cause and Effect organizer on page 145. Have them write in the top right box the effect: *Mrs. Blue felt better.* Then have them review the book to locate a cause for this effect. Give students other examples from the book, alternating cause and effect examples so students can practice figuring out what happened in the story and why these things happened.

64B

Tug, Tug, Tug

An African Folk Tale

retold by Linda Yoshizawa
Leveled Reader 64B
Genre: Folk Tale
Level: Easy/Average

Summary

When Turtle is forced first by Hippo, and then by Elephant, to leave the pond, he makes a plan. Turtle challenges each large animal separately to a tug-of-war. They each agree that if Turtle wins, they will share the pond with him. Unknown to Hippo and Elephant, Turtle gives each of them one end of the same vine. The two big animals get exhausted pulling against each other, each thinking they are pulling against Turtle. Finally they are forced to agree that they will share the pond with Turtle.

At a Glance

Links to the Student Edition

⟳ **Comprehension Skill:** Cause and Effect

Selection Vocabulary: *discovered, poems, secret*

Program Theme: Myself and Others
Unit Theme: Finding My Place

You can overcome opponents who are bigger and stronger than you by using your brains and outsmarting them.

Before Reading

Motivating the Reader
Build Background About Tug-of-War

Tie a handkerchief around the middle of a long jump rope and create two lines a few feet apart on the floor with masking tape. Have teams play tug-of-war, trying to pull the handkerchief over the line nearest them. Arrange students to create both equal and unequal teams. Have observing students predict which team will win. Then ask students to imagine a tug-of-war between a hippo and a turtle, an elephant and a turtle, and a hippo and an elephant. Have students predict the outcome of each tug-of-war.

Preview and Predict

Have students scan the cover, text, and illustrations to get an idea of what the book is about. Let the students know that this is a trickster tale. Discuss with students the characteristics of a trickster tale—where one character, often a smaller and weaker animal, uses clever thinking to outsmart a bigger character. Have students open the book so they can see both front and back covers, and ask them to predict which of the three animals is the trickster. Suggest students read to find out how the trickster character will fool the other characters.

Point out selection vocabulary and any unfamiliar words, such as *floated, grumbling, doze, settle,* and *budge,* that might be important to understanding the story.

During Reading

Guiding Comprehension

Use the following questions to support students as they read.

- **Pages 2–3 What made the "ground" shake under Turtle?** (Turtle was on Hippo's back. When Hippo moved, Turtle thought the ground under him was shaking.)

- **Pages 4–5 Why did Turtle get out of the pond when Hippo told him to go?** (Hippo was very big, and Turtle was very little.)

- **Page 7 How does Turtle feel? What clues help you figure this out?** (He is angry and upset. He grumbles and he says that making him leave the pond isn't fair.)

- **Page 7 What does Turtle mean when he says he has a big brain?** (He means he is smart.)

- **Pages 8–9 Why did Elephant think he could easily win a tug-of-war?** (Elephant was much bigger and stronger than Turtle.)

- **Pages 10–11 What do you think will happen next?** (Each of the big animals has one end of the vine. They will probably have a tug-of-war against each other without knowing it.)

- **Page 12 What does _budge_ mean in this sentence? How do you know?** (In a tug-of-war, both sides try to pull the other side closer. _Budge_ means to move.)

- **Page 14 Why wouldn't Hippo and Elephant give in?** (Each thought he was pulling against little Turtle and was ashamed to lose to him. They just couldn't believe that Turtle was so strong.)

- **Page 15 What happens once Elephant and Hippo give up?** (They now have to share the pond with Turtle.)

- **Page 16 Do Hippo and Elephant know that Turtle tricked them? Which words help you figure this out?** (No, they don't know about Turtle's trick. The words _still wonder_ and _secret_ are clues that help me figure this out.)

Reading Strategies

If... a student does not understand what Turtle means when he says he has a big brain,	**Then...** explain that Turtle means he can outthink the other animals even if he is smaller and weaker than they are.
If... a student has trouble explaining Turtle's trick,	**Then...** have the student reread page 12 and describe the illustration.
If... a student cannot recognize cause-and-effect relationships,	**Then...** use **Model Your Thinking** below.

Model Your Thinking

 Comprehension Skill: Cause and Effect

To better understand a story, good readers think about what happens in a story and why it happens. An effect is what happens; a cause is why it happens. On page 4, I read that Turtle leaves the pond. That's an effect. To find the cause, I ask myself: "Why did Turtle leave the pond?" He left because Hippo, who is bigger and stronger than Turtle, told him to go away. As I keep reading, I keep asking myself "What happened?" and "Why did it happen?" to help me find other causes and effects in the story.

After Reading

Revisiting the Text

Comprehension Use the Cause and Effect organizer on page 145. Fill in a cause or an effect in each row of the organizer. Have students complete the organizer by rereading the book to find the appropriate cause or effect. More fluent readers can use a blank organizer and fill in both causes and effects.

65A
Ice Walk

by Cass Hollander
Leveled Reader 65A
Genre: Realistic Story
Level: Easy

Summary

Ma, Pa, Nellie, and George like to cross the river on foot when the river is frozen solid. But this time, although they are told it is safe, it turns out to be dangerous. The ice begins to crack just as Ma and Nellie are going across. After Ma gets them safely across, the family warns others that the ice is no longer safe.

At a Glance

Links to the Student Edition

 Comprehension Skill: Character

Selection Vocabulary: *basketball, bounced, playground, aimed*

Program Theme: Myself and Others
Unit Theme: Finding My Place

Part of being brave is to consider others who face the same danger as you do. A mother's bravery helps her and her child cross the cracking ice.

Before Reading

Motivating the Reader
Build Background About Character Traits

Display two or three pictures of familiar book, movie, or TV characters. Have students brainstorm words that describe each character, and list students' descriptive words under each picture. Then ask them to predict what each character might do in a special situation, such as seeing a fire or an automobile accident. Ask the students to explain their answers.

Preview and Predict

Have students scan the cover, text, and illustrations to get an idea of what the book is about. Prepare them to read by drawing their attention to the book's cover. Ask them to read the title and describe what these two people are doing. Encourage students to make predictions about what might happen in the book.

Point out selection vocabulary and any unfamiliar words, such as *hailed, ferry,* and *telegraphed,* that might be important to understanding the book.

During Reading

Guiding Comprehension

Use the following questions to support students as they read.

- **Pages 2–3** *Why does the author compare the ice walk to a playground?* (Both are fun; children can run and slide and play on the ice.)

- **Page 4** *Why does the family look for breaks or cracks in the ice?* (A person might fall into the river if he or she stepped on or near a break or crack in the ice.)

- **Pages 4–5** *What did the man mean when he said he could have bounced a basketball on the ice? How do you know?* (He meant the ice was hard. You need a hard surface to bounce a ball.)

- **Page 6** *Why does Pa like to go first? What does this action tell you about him?* (He likes to go first to make sure the ice is safe for the whole family. This action shows that he is a caring father and husband.)

- **Pages 9–10** *How is Nellie feeling? How do you know?* (She is very frightened. She goes stiff with fear, her heart bounces, she has trouble breathing, and she begins to cry.)

- **Pages 10–11** *What do you think Ma will do next? Why do you think so?* (Answers will vary, but students will likely predict that Ma will keep moving ahead with Nellie until they reach safety.)

- **Page 11** *What were the noises that Nellie and Ma heard?* (The noises were the sounds of the ice breaking up.)

- **Page 13** *What do you think Ma and Pa will do next? Why do you think so?* (Ma and Pa will probably make sure that others are warned about the ice. At the end of page 13 Ma says, "We must spread the word.")

- **Page 15** *Why does the station master telegraph a message to the other side of the river?* (People on the other side of the river wouldn't know that the ice wasn't safe.)

Reading Strategies

If...	Then...
If... a student does not understand what the danger is when ice melts on a frozen river,	**Then...** have him or her examine the illustrations. Explain that the water under the ice is very cold.
If... a student has trouble with the word *telegraphed*,	**Then...** explain that the telegraph was a way people sent messages before phones were invented.
If... a student has difficulty drawing conclusions about characters,	**Then...** use **Model Your Thinking** below.

Model Your Thinking

 Comprehension Skill: Character

 Think ALOUD

A character is a person or animal in a story. As I read, I pay attention to how the author describes what a character thinks, says, and does. Good readers use these clues to figure out what the characters are like. On page 9, I read that Nellie grows stiff with fear, but that Ma doesn't let go of her hand. Nellie's actions tell me that she is very frightened. Ma's actions and words show that she stays calm in a dangerous situation. Despite her fear, Ma makes sure she and Nellie get across safely. Ma is very brave.

After Reading

Revisiting the Text

Comprehension Use Web 1 on page 132. Have students choose one of the characters in the book and list details about what that person says and does. Have students write one or two sentences underneath their webs that tell what the character is like and why they think so.

65B
My Favorite Sport

by Judy Nayer
Leveled Reader 65B
Genre: Rhyme
Level: Easy/Average

Summary

In this upbeat rhyming story, Tanya watches and keeps score for her father and brother as they play basketball. Then, one day, she decides she would like to play basketball too. She surprisingly finds it easy to do and fun. She practices every day and becomes a better and better player. When Dad recognizes her determination and skill, he gives her a basketball of her own. Now, Tanya, Rick, and Dad all play together.

At a Glance

Links to the Student Edition

☞ **Comprehension Skill:** Character

Selection Vocabulary: *basketball, shoot, gift*

Program Theme: Myself and Others
Unit Theme: Finding My Place

Watching other people play a sport can be fun, but sometimes it's even better when you learn to play too.

Before Reading

Motivating the Reader
Build Background About Basketball

Take a class survey to find out how many students play basketball and how many know about professional and local teams. If possible, show photographs or videotape of both male and female basketball players. Then list on the chalkboard the skills the students think are needed to be a good basketball player.

Preview and Predict

Have students scan the cover, text, and illustrations to get an idea of what the book is about. Read a few lines of text, and have students note the rhyme pattern. Encourage students to make predictions about what happens to the characters. Suggest students set their own purpose for reading, such as find out why basketball is Tanya's favorite sport.

Point out selection vocabulary and any unfamiliar words, especially those related to basketball such as *court, one-on-one, swish, jump shot, dribble,* and *slam-dunk,* that might be important to understanding the book. You may wish to have volunteers demonstrate or describe these terms for the other students.

During Reading

Guiding Comprehension

Use the following questions to support students as they read.

- **Pages 2–3** *Who are the main characters of this book?* (Rick, Tanya, Dad)

- **Pages 2–3** *What game do Rick and Dad play?* (basketball)

- **Page 3** *Who is telling this story? How do you know?* (Tanya is telling the story. Dad says, "Hi, Tanya." This means *me* refers to Tanya.)

- **Pages 3–4** *What does "one-on-one" mean? Break this phrase into smaller words and look at the pictures.* (It means two players, playing against each other.)

- **Page 4** *What does Tanya do while Dad and Rick play?* (She keeps track of the score.)

- **Pages 4–5** *What do you think Tanya is feeling? What do you think she will do next?* (Tanya wishes she could join in the action. She will try to play basketball.)

- **Pages 6–7** *How do you think Tanya feels at this point in the book?* (Tanya may feel surprised at her own ability. She enjoys playing and feels proud and happy.)

- **Pages 9–11** *How do you think Dad feels as he watches Tanya?* (He is surprised at her skill and is proud of her.)

- **Page 13** *What does Dad mean when he says, "I really should have known."?* (Possible answers: He should have realized Tanya would like to play too. He should have known she would be a good player.)

- **Page 16** *How is this game different from the game described on pages 4 and 5?* (Tanya now plays with her dad and Rick.)

Reading Strategies

If... a student misses the pattern of the rhyming lines,	**Then...** model for the student an appropriate way to read a poem.
If... a student has difficulty seeing how Tanya changes during the story,	**Then...** have the student compare the picture on pages 4–5 to the picture on page 16.
If... a student has difficulty drawing conclusions about characters,	**Then...** use **Model Your Thinking** below.

Model Your Thinking

Think ALOUD

Comprehension Skill: Character

A character is a person or animal in a story. To figure out what a character is like, good readers pay attention to how the author describes what the character says, thinks, and does. On page 5, we read that Tanya wishes she could play. Then we see how hard she practices each day. Her words and the exclamation points show she is really having fun. On page 10, Dad's words show that he thinks she's a good player. I admire Tanya for trying something new and working so hard to be a good player. Thinking about characters helps me understand the story better.

After Reading

Revisiting the Text

Comprehension Have students use the T-Chart on page 150 to analyze Tanya's character. Students can list words that describe her on the left side of the chart and give reasons to support their thinking on the right side. Have students then use their charts to draw a picture and write a paragraph about Tanya.

66A
Bumbles

by Deborah Eaton
Leveled Reader 66A
Genre: Informational Article
Level: Easy

Summary

A fat black and yellow bumblebee buzzes about on a spring day. She is the queen looking for a nest. Readers follow her into her new nest. They learn about the annual cycle of egg-laying, the hatching of the bees, their work through the summer, and their deaths in the fall.

At a Glance

Links to the Student Edition

⊙ **Comprehension Skill:** Graphic Sources

Selection Vocabulary: *collect, insects, plants, hinge*

Program Theme: The World Around Us
Unit Theme: The Whole Wide World

Follow the queen bee back to her nest to learn more about the world of bees.

Before Reading

Motivating the Reader
Build Background About Describing Insects

Ask students to close their eyes and think about what they hear and smell. Have them feel their desktops. Point out that we not only experience things by seeing them, but by hearing, feeling, smelling, and sometimes tasting them as well. Draw symbols on the chalkboard for the five senses. Have pairs think of a familiar insect and complete the Five-Column Chart on page 153, listing sensory details about their insect. Encourage students to pay attention to how the author describes bumblebees as they read the book.

Preview and Predict

Have students scan the cover, text, and illustrations to get an idea of what the book is about. Draw their attention to the book's cover. Read the title and say:

> This article is going to give you a closer look at something familiar. What do you think it will be?

Have students preview the rest of the pictures to predict the places and activities the book will show. Students can set their own purpose for reading, such as finding out where bumblebees live.

Point out the selection vocabulary and any unfamiliar words, such as *queen, nest,* and *nectar,* that might be important to understanding the book.

During Reading

Guiding Comprehension

Use the following questions to support students as they read.

- **Pages 2–3** Humans have five senses: sight, hearing, smell, taste, and feeling, or touch. **What three senses does the author use in describing the scene? Give an example of each.** (She says the sun feels warm. She describes the sight of bright yellow dandelions. She describes the *bzzzzz* sound of the bee.)

- **Page 3** **What do you think this book is about? What clues help you figure this out?** (The word *BZZZZ* and the picture suggests the book is about bees.)

- **Page 5** **What does this picture show? What do the labels tell you?** (It is a picture of a bumblebee. The labels tell you the different parts of a bumblebee.)

- **Pages 5–6** **If you see a bumblebee in spring, what type is it? How do you know?** (It is a queen. Only queens are alive in the spring.)

- **Pages 6–7** **What are queen bees doing in the spring?** (They are looking for nests.)

- **Page 8** **Where do wild bumblebees live?** (in nests in the ground) **What are their nests like?** (a dark hole in the ground, such as an old mouse's nest or an old chipmunk nest)

- **Pages 9–11** **What does the queen do during the first weeks in her nest?** (She makes a honey pot, fills the honey pot with nectar, lays eggs, and sips nectar.)

- **Page 12** **How are the workers related to the queen?** (They are her children.)

- **Pages 13–14** **What do the workers and the queen do all summer?** (Workers gather food from flowers and carry it to the nest. The queen lays eggs.)

- **Pages 14–15** **When the cold fall comes, what happens to the bees?** (Workers and old queens die. Young queens live over the winter.)

Reading Strategies

If... a student has difficulty reading *BZZZZ* on page 3,	**Then...** point out that the word is meant to imitate a sound.
If... a student has difficulty comprehending how a wing is like a hinge,	**Then...** point out a door's hinges and demonstrate how they allow the door to open and close.
If... a student has difficulty interpreting graphic sources, such as a diagram,	**Then...** use **Model Your Thinking** below.

Model Your Thinking

Think ALOUD

Comprehension Skill: Graphic Sources

Graphic sources can be pictures, diagrams, maps, charts, graphs, or something else that shows information in an easy-to-see way. I study graphic sources carefully because they give important information and help me understand what I read. This book doesn't say much about a bumblebee's body, but the diagram on page 5 gives lots of information. It makes some of the book's ideas much clearer. For example, the author talks about the queen bee's long tongue, and I can see it labeled clearly in the diagram. The words and the pictures help me better understand how the queen bee uses her tongue to get nectar.

After Reading

Revisiting the Text

Comprehension Direct students to the picture on page 11. Have them reread pages 8–11 with a partner, comparing the text with picture details. Have them use self-sticking notes to label the illustration. Suggest they label the *nest, queen, eggs,* and *honey pot.* Repeat with other illustrations, or have students draw and label their own pictures.

66B

Seed Surprises

by Andrew Willet
Leveled Reader 66B
Genre: Informational Article
Level: Easy/Average

Summary

A tiny seed grows into a giant tree. It is one of nature's surprises! This book shows different seed types and describes the ways plants spread their seeds. Readers learn how soil, sunlight, wind, water, animals, and humans do their share to help seeds grow.

At a Glance

Links to the Student Edition

ℭ **Comprehension Skill:** Graphic Sources

Selection Vocabulary: *plants, trap, pitcher, hinge*

Program Theme: The World Around Us
Unit Theme: The Whole Wide World

Every plant we see around us starts from a seed. Some seeds go on amazing trips before they take root in the ground.

Before Reading

Motivating the Reader
Build Background About Seeds

Display types of seeds that look quite different from each other, such as sunflower seeds, acorns, avocado pits, lima beans, and apple seeds. Crack open a nut to show a seed and its covering. Discuss the kinds of plants that would grow, under the right conditions, from each seed. Draw a web on the chalkboard similar to Web 2 on page 133. In the center circle, write: *What makes seeds grow?* Have students suggest answers to the question, such as *soil, sunlight, warmth,* and *water.* Record their answers in the web's outer circles. Encourage students to think about what they know about seeds and plants as they read the book.

Preview and Predict

Have students scan the cover, text, and illustrations to get an idea of what the book is about. Draw their attention to the title. Ask them to predict what surprising things about seeds they might find out in the book. Encourage students to think of some questions about seeds and to read to find out the answers to their questions.

Point out the selection vocabulary and any unfamiliar words, such as *scatter, propellers, acorns,* and *thorny,* that might be important to understanding the book.

During Reading

Guiding Comprehension

Use the following questions to support students as they read.

- **Page 2** *In what ways are types of seeds different from each other?* (They are different shapes and sizes.) *How are all seeds alike?* (They can all grow into new plants.)

- **Pages 4–5** *What are two things seeds need to grow?* (They need space and light.)

- **Page 6** *What is another word that means almost the same as scatter?* (spread) *How does wind help scatter, or spread, dandelion seeds?* (The wind blows the light seeds to new places.)

- **Page 7** *Why does the author say maple seeds look like airplane propellers?* (Like propellers, maple seeds have long blades that catch the wind. These blades help the seed fly like a propeller helps a plane fly.)

- **Pages 8–9** *How are new palm trees created?* (Some coconuts of old palm trees fall into the water and are carried by waves to a beach. The coconuts are seeds from which new palm trees grow.) *What does the picture in this small circle show?* (It shows a new palm tree sprouting from a coconut.)

- **Pages 10–11** *How might a bird and a squirrel help new plants grow?* (A bird might eat a fruit with a seed in it. It might toss out the seed or leave the seed behind in its waste. A squirrel may bury an acorn and forget about it.)

- **Pages 12–13** *How does the witch hazel plant spread its seeds?* (The seeds are held in little cases. When the cases dry out and split open, the seeds pop out and are thrown away from the old plant.)

- **Pages 14–15** *How do thorny seeds get spread?* (They are sticky and catch a ride on animals' fur or people's clothing.)

- **Page 16** *What are four ways seeds travel?* (They can be carried by wind, water, or animals. Some pop from their plants.)

Reading Strategies

If... a student has difficulty comprehending information in the book,	**Then...** encourage the student to pause often to think about the main idea of a page by asking: "What is this page all about?"
If... a student has difficulty interpreting graphic sources, such as photographs,	**Then...** use **Model Your Thinking** below.

Model Your Thinking

 Comprehension Skill: Graphic Sources

Some books use pictures, charts, diagrams, or maps to give more information or to help make the ideas in the text clearer. Graphic sources show information in an easy-to-see way that helps me understand what I read. The photographs in this book help me better understand the different ways seeds travel. I can read about how the witch hazel plant throws its seeds on pages 12 and 13, but the picture of the seeds popping out of their case helps me understand this process better. I can also make my own graphic sources to help me understand and remember what I've read. For example, I could draw pictures or make a word web or table to show the different ways seeds travel to new places.

After Reading

Revisiting the Text

Comprehension Organize students into small groups. Have each group pick a plant from the book and reread the text to find out how the plant spreads its seeds. Have groups draw pictures showing this process and write labels or captions to explain it. Display students' drawings on a bulletin board entitled: *How Plants Spread Their Seeds.*

67A
Annie's Plants

by Babs Bell Hajdusiewicz
Leveled Reader 67A
Genre: Rhyme
Level: Easy

Summary

Annie wants some little plants in her room, but plants don't stay little for long. Annie's plants grow so large that they tickle her head in the night. Annie does not give up. She buys new plants and tries again. Finally, she finds a clever way to let her plants grow and get some sleep too. She goes to bed wearing a helmet.

At a Glance

Links to the Student Edition

 Comprehension Skill: Realism and Fantasy

Selection Vocabulary: *dream, scary*

Program Theme: The World Around Us
Unit Theme: The Whole Wide World

A child's bedroom can be the most important place in the whole world. So when plants take over Annie's bedroom, she needs to find a solution fast.

Before Reading

Motivating the Reader
Build Background About Rhyming

Invite students to think of topics they've read about lately. Work with them to select one topic and write it in the center of Web 3 on page 134. Ask students to suggest five words related to the topic and write them in the circles closest to the web's center. Work together to add rhyming words in the outer circles along each line. Model completing one line of the web. For example, if the topic were *Bees,* the first word on a line might be *queen.* Other circles along the line might contain the words *green, mean,* and *screen.* Invite students to use some of the web words in short poems. Encourage students to look for rhyming words as they read the book.

Preview and Predict

Have students scan the cover, text, and illustrations to get an idea of what the book is about. Select volunteers to read pages 2–4 aloud, and have students listen for rhyming words. Ask students to describe Annie's problem and make predictions about how she will try to solve it. Encourage them to read to see if their predictions are correct.

Point out the selection vocabulary and any unfamiliar words, such as *stretched, tickled,* and *helmet,* that might be important to understanding the book.

During Reading

Guiding Comprehension

Use the following questions to support students as they read.

- **Page 2** *Where does Annie put her plants?* (beside her bed—some on the floor and another on the windowsill)

- **Page 2** *Which sentences have rhyming words? Which words rhyme?* (The second and fourth sentences end with the rhyming words *bed* and *said*.)

- **Page 3** *What happens to Annie's plants?* (They grow big and stretch across her bed.)

- **Page 4** *What is Annie's problem?* (She can't sleep at night because plants tickle her head.)

- **Pages 5–7** *How does Annie try to solve her problem?* (She takes the big plants outside and buys more small ones, which she puts by her bed.)

- **Page 8** *Restate the third sentence in your own words.* (Annie had a nightmare.)

- **Page 9** *What do you think will happen next?* (The plants will grow like other plants and tickle Annie's head when she tries to sleep.)

- **Page 11** *What happens to each new set of plants that Annie buys?* (Each set grows too big, and they tickle her head.)

- **Page 11** *Do you think Annie's plants are like the plants you see in the real world? Why or why not?* (No. Real plants can't grow this much in one night.)

- **Page 13** *What kind of store do picture clues tell you is next to the plant store?* (The sign saying "Sports" suggests it is a sporting goods store.)

- **Page 14** *What do you think is in the bag on Annie's bed?* (Predictions may vary. Some students may use the picture of a helmet on page 12 to predict she will protect her head from the tickling plants by wearing a helmet.)

- **Page 16** *How does Annie finally solve her problem?* (She wears a helmet to bed so the growing plants can't tickle her head.)

Reading Strategies

If... a student cannot recognize the rhyme and rhythm in this story through silent reading,

Then... have that student read aloud or listen as a partner reads to hear rhyming words and rhythm.

If... a student makes good predictions,

Then... praise the student for using story clues and recognizing repetition to tell what will happen next.

If... a student has trouble distinguishing events that could really happen and events that could not really happen,

Then... use **Model Your Thinking** below.

Model Your Thinking

Think ALOUD

Comprehension Skill: Realism and Fantasy

Realistic stories tell about things that could happen in real life. A fantasy includes some things that could really happen and some things that couldn't really happen. At first, the events in *Annie's Plants* seem realistic. A girl could really buy plants and put them in her room. But I notice that the author tells the story in rhyme. Many fantasy stories I've read use rhyme, so this gives me the idea that some strange things may happen. Sure enough, I soon read about plants quickly growing so big that they stretch across Annie's bed and tickle her head. In real life, plants can't grow this fast. This event tells me *Annie's Plants* is a fantasy, not a realistic story.

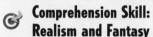

After Reading

Revisiting the Text

Comprehension Have pairs use the Plot/Story Sequence organizer on page 137 to record important story events and identify each one as something that could or couldn't happen in real life. Pairs can draw pictures to show these events.

67B

Your New Planet

by Richard C. Lawrence
Leveled Reader 67B
Genre: Fantasy
Level: Easy/Average

Summary

Three "space kids" act as narrators to welcome readers on an outer space journey. They offer helpful hints for traveling to and visiting a new planet. With suggestions such as "Try to get a window seat!" and "Act cool!," the narrators have plenty of advice for future space kids.

At a Glance

Links to the Student Edition

☞ **Comprehension Skill:** Realism and Fantasy

Selection Vocabulary: *space, spaceship, planet, breathe*

Program Theme: The World Around Us
Unit Theme: The Whole Wide World

The world widens as this fantasy takes readers into outer space to visit a new planet.

Before Reading

Motivating the Reader
Build Background about Visiting New Places

Encourage students to think about the most unusual place they have visited. Suggest that it can be as far away as a foreign country or as near as a neighbor's attic. Ask them to combine pictures and words to make a travel poster showing special features of the place. Volunteers can display their posters and share stories about their travels.

Preview and Predict

Have students scan the cover, text, and illustrations to get an idea of what the book is about. Have a volunteer read aloud pages 2 and 3. Have students tell who is telling the story and where and when it takes place. Ask them to use word and pictures clues to decide whether this book tells about real people and events or is a make-believe story. Then encourage students to make predictions about what will happen in the book. Then have students set their own purpose for reading, such as finding out what the story tells about outer space.

Point out the selection vocabulary and any unfamiliar words, such as *moons, stars, sun,* and *space suit,* that might be important to understanding the book.

During Reading

Guiding Comprehension

Use the following questions to support students as they read.

- **Page 2** According to the story and the picture clues, who is telling this story? (The narrators are three kids who call themselves Kids in Space.)

- **Page 3** What are the Space Kids going to do? (They will show people how to be happy on a new planet.)

- **Pages 4–5** What two space travel hints do the Space Kids offer? (Don't be late for your spaceship and don't take too much stuff.)

- **Page 5** Are books in this story like most books you've read? Explain. (No. The books in the story all fit on a small machine that looks like a computer. Most books I've read are made of paper.)

- **Page 6** Where do the Space Kids think you should sit on the spaceship? (on a seat near a window) Why? (So you can see great things in the sky, such as moons, stars, and planets.)

- **Page 8** What do you think it means to act cool? (It means "to act unexcited, like something is not a big deal.")

- **Page 9** Why will you need a space suit and helmet when going outside on your new planet? (You will need them to breathe.)

- **Pages 11–12** How do the Space Kids compare playing ball on Earth with playing ball on other planets? (On some planets you would be lighter than on Earth. You could jump, throw, or kick better than on Earth. On a big planet, you would weigh more and it would be harder to run or jump.)

- **Page 14** Which kind of planet would you like to live on—one where you are lighter than you are on Earth or heavier? Why? (Encourage well-supported answers.)

- **Page 16** What is one thing all Kids in Space have in common? (They all talk and dream about Earth.)

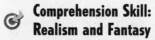
Reading Strategies

If... a student confuses *breathe* with *breath* on page 9,	**Then...** model each word and have the student decide which one makes the most sense.
If... a student cannot tell that this book is a fantasy,	**Then...** use **Model Your Thinking** below.

Model Your Thinking

Comprehension Skill: Realism and Fantasy

Think ALOUD

A realistic story tells about things that could really happen. A fantasy includes some things that could really happen and some things that couldn't really happen. I know this story is a fantasy because it tells about things that couldn't really happen. At the present time, people cannot travel into space to live on new planets. The pictures were my first clue that this book is a fantasy. I saw spaceships and space suits. I saw buildings and vehicles that looked like they were from a future time. The fact that the pictures looked more like cartoons than realistic drawings or photographs is also a clue that this book is a fantasy.

After Reading

Revisiting the Text

Comprehension Use the T-Chart on page 150. On the left side, write *Real-Life Events*. On the right side, write *Events on Your New Planet*. Help students list real-life events related to those in the story, such as traveling, driving outside, playing ball, and running track. Have students reread the book and record how similar events are described in the book.

68A
Do Animals Know?

by Kathy Mormile
Leveled Reader 68A
Genre: Informational Article
Level: Easy

Summary

Can animals predict the weather? The author suggests that animal behaviors often foretell weather events. When a storm is brewing, rabbits hide in the woods. Sea crabs move inland. While people rely on scientific equipment to forecast weather, animals use their instincts.

At a Glance

Links to the Student Edition

☞ **Comprehension Skill:** Context Clues

Selection Vocabulary: *noise, warnings*

Program Theme: The World Around Us
Unit Theme: The Whole Wide World

The whole wide world is affected by weather. Many animals can sense severe weather and take action. By watching them, we can predict whether a storm is likely.

Before Reading

Motivating the Reader
Build Background about Weather

Write *Sunshine, Rain, Storm, Snow* on the chalkboard. Draw a symbol for each type of weather. Ask students to describe what each type of weather is like and what people should or shouldn't do during each type of weather. List their responses on the chalkboard. As students prepare to read the book, encourage them to think about how animals act in different kinds of weather.

Preview and Predict

Have students scan the cover, text, and illustrations to get an idea of what the book is about. Encourage them to name the animals they see. Invite a volunteer to read aloud pages 2–3. Encourage students to make predictions on how animals may tell us if it's going to rain. Suggest students read to find out what animals may know about the weather.

Point out the selection vocabulary and any unfamiliar words, such as *storm, protect,* and *harm,* that might be important to understanding the book.

During Reading

Guiding Comprehension

Use the following questions to support students as they read.

- **Page 4** What may cause animals to act differently when a storm is near? (Animals may react to air changes.)

- **Pages 4–8** Why do you think some animals make a lot of noise before a storm? (They are probably giving warning to others to take cover.)

- **Page 6** What warnings do animals get that tell them a storm is coming? (Before a storm, they hear low sounds that people can't hear.)

- **Page 7** What do animals look for when they think a storm is coming? (They seek a safe, dry place.)

- **Page 8** How can you tell from watching bats that bad weather may be coming? (They screech loudly before a storm and sometimes fly into buildings.) Repeat this question for other animals.

- **Page 9** How do you think trees and plants can protect rabbits during a storm? (They can hide under trees and plants and stay dry and warm.)

- **Page 10** Why is land safer for sea crabs than the water during a storm? (Storms create strong waves in the sea that could hurt the crabs if they stayed in the water.)

- **Page 13** What might happen if a butterfly didn't hide under a leaf during a heavy rain storm? (The rain could hurt its wings.)

- **Page 15** Why do birds rest on wires before a storm? (The air is thin before a storm. Thin air makes it hard for birds to fly.)

- **Page 16** Why should you check with animals before planning a party outside? (Animals can tell if bad weather is coming. By watching them, you can predict whether you'll have good weather for an outdoor party.)

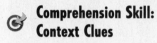

Ongoing Assessment

Reading Strategies

If...	Then...
If... a student does not understand the effects a coming storm has on animal behavior,	**Then...** help the student use the Cause and Effect organizer on page 145.
If... a student can explain how animals can help people predict bad weather,	**Then...** praise the student for identifying the main idea.
If... a student has trouble using context clues,	**Then...** use **Model Your Thinking** below.

Model Your Thinking

Think ALOUD

- **Comprehension Skill: Context Clues**

I can often figure out the meaning of a new word by looking at the words and phrases around it. I can also use pictures as clues. For example, I can figure out what warnings *means on page 6 by looking at other words in the sentence and reading the following sentence. These context clues tell me that sounds tell animals a storm is coming. These sounds are warnings. I think warnings are something that tells you when something bad is about to happen. I can check my definition in a dictionary or a glossary to be sure.*

After Reading

Revisiting the Text

Comprehension Use the Vocabulary Frame on page 136. Assign pairs a word from the book. Have them write the word in the top left box and draw a picture they associate with the word in the top right box. Have pairs predict a meaning for the word and use the word in a sentence about the book. Then have pairs use context clues in the book to verify the meaning and write a second sentence. If students are still unsure, have them check a dictionary.

68B
The Storm

by Judy Nayer
Leveled Reader 68B
Genre: Realistic Story
Level: Easy/Average

Summary

Dark skies and heavy clouds tell Matt a storm is on the way. The radio warns that a tornado watch is in effect. When the tornado hits, Matt and his mother are safe in the basement, but Lucky is outside. Matt is happy to find his "lucky" dog has made it through the tornado safely. Despite the damage the tornado caused, everyone feels lucky to have survived it.

At a Glance

Links to the Student Edition

⌖ **Comprehension Skill:** Context Clues

Selection Vocabulary: *storms, destroy, powerful, wrecked*

**Program Theme: The World Around Us
Unit Theme: The Whole Wide World**

Severe storms, such as tornadoes, threaten every region in the world. People all over the world have learned to prepare for such storms and protect themselves.

Before Reading

Motivating the Reader
Build Background about Tornadoes

Discuss any experiences students may have had with violent storms. Display a U.S. map. Point out the Tornado Alley that includes parts of Kansas, Iowa, Missouri, Arkansas, Nebraska, Oklahoma, and Texas. Have students find their own region on the map and see where they live in relation to the Tornado Alley. Then write *Tornado* in the center of Web 1 on page 132. Have students add words and phrases they connect to a tornado, such as *twister, funnel, roar, destroys,* and *lifts houses.*

Preview and Predict

Have students scan the cover, text, and illustrations. Read the book title together. Then ask students to use the illustrations to make predictions. Ask:

> What type of storm will this be? Who are the main characters who will face it? What do you think will happen during the storm?

Encourage students to read to find out whether their predictions are correct, revising them if necessary.

Point out the selection vocabulary and any unfamiliar words, such as *tornado, drills, funnel,* and *survived,* that might be important to understanding the book.

During Reading

Guiding Comprehension

Use the following questions to support students as they read.

- **Page 2** **What clues help you understand where Matt lives?** (The phrase "running across the field" suggests Matt lives in the country rather than a city. The picture shows grain fields and his home is a farmhouse style.)

- **Page 3** **How did Lucky get his name?** (As a puppy, he luckily missed getting run over.)

- **Page 6** **What makes Matt decide a storm is coming?** (It is dark. There are heavy clouds.)

- **Page 7** **Do you think Matt lives in a place where tornadoes might happen? Why or why not?** (Students should conclude the region often has tornadoes because Matt knows about them and his school holds tornado drills.)

- **Page 8** **What does a tornado watch mean?** (It means there is a chance a tornado could happen.)

- **Page 10** **What words help you imagine how a tornado moves and what it sounds like?** (Students should point to *funnel, twisting like a snake,* and *whistling* as details that help them visualize a tornado.)

- **Page 11** **What happens on this page?** (Lucky is out in the storm. Matt and his mom go into the basement.)

- **Page 12** **What does *powerful* mean? What other word would make sense in this sentence?** (strong)

- **Page 15** **What happened to Lucky?** (He went inside his doghouse. The tornado picked up his doghouse and blew it into a neighbor's yard, but Lucky wasn't hurt.) **Do you think Lucky is a fitting name for Matt's dog? Why or why not?** (Students will probably say the name fits because Lucky seems to escape trouble every time he is in danger.)

Reading Strategies

If... a student has difficulty telling the difference between a character's words and the story narration,	**Then...** point out the use of paragraph indentation and quotation marks.
If... a student is unfamiliar with *funnel* and cannot use the word to visualize a tornado,	**Then...** draw a funnel on the chalkboard or show a real funnel.
If... a student has trouble using context clues,	**Then...** use **Model Your Thinking** below.

Model Your Thinking

 Comprehension Skill: Context Clues

When I come across a new word, I often find clues to its meaning in nearby words or sentences. These clues are called context clues. On page 12, I see the word *crouched.* I read the phrase "under the table" and understand that to *crouch* I would squat or bend down low and make myself small. The picture on page 12 also helps me understand the meaning of *crouched.* If I am still not sure what the word means, then I can check a dictionary or glossary.

After Reading

Revisiting the Text

Comprehension Use the Three-Column Chart on page 151. Across the top of the chart, write the heads *Unfamiliar Word, Context Clues,* and *Meaning.* Give students words from the book or have them self-select some. Have pairs complete the chart by rereading the book and using context clues to figure out the meaning of the words. Then invite students to draw a picture or write a sentence for the word they found most challenging.

69A
Amber
The Golden Trap

by Dona R. McDuff
Leveled Reader 69A
Genre: Informational Article
Level: Easy

Summary

Amber has been used in jewelry for thousands of years. It is also an important material in scientific study. The amber we see today started out long ago as tree sap. When the sap hardened into amber, it often trapped plants, animals, and insects, preserving them as clues to the past.

At a Glance

Links to the Student Edition

⌖ **Comprehension Skill:** Fact and Opinion

Selection Vocabulary: *thousands, ocean*

Program Theme: The World Around Us
Unit Theme: The Whole Wide World

Scientists can not only tell us about the world around us today, they can also tell us about the world long ago. Amber is a golden trap which has caught and preserved things that lived thousands of years ago.

Before Reading

Motivating the Reader
Build Background About Archaeology

Display pictures of fossils, dinosaur bones, and creatures caught in amber. Explain that scientists can use objects like these to find out more about what life was like millions of years ago. Invite students to imagine spending ten minutes with a dinosaur. Have them work in pairs to write five questions they would ask their dinosaur about its world. Invite pairs to read their questions aloud.

Preview and Predict

Have students scan the cover, text, and illustrations to get an idea of what the book is about. Have students use word and picture clues to predict why amber is called "the golden trap." Draw their attention to pictures of dinosaurs, ants, and scientists. Suggest they read to find out what each of these has to do with amber.

Point out the selection vocabulary and any unfamiliar words, such as *trap, clues, sap,* and *sticky,* that might be important to understanding the book.

During Reading

Guiding Comprehension

Use the following questions to support students as they read.

- **Page 2** *Have you ever heard of amber? What do you know about it?* (Students should tell what they already know.)

- **Page 3** *How is amber used in the pictures on this page?* (Amber is used in jewelry.)

- **Pages 4–6** *The book names four things scientists look at to study the past. What are they?* (They look at bones, footprints, leaf prints, and amber.)

- **Page 7** *What do you think will happen next?* (The ant will get stuck in the tree sap.)

- **Page 9** *How is amber created?* (It starts out as tree sap that hardens and turns into amber.)

- **Page 9** *Why is tree sap a good insect trap?* (Tree sap is sticky.) *How old could this ant be? How do you know?* (It could be millions of years old because that is how long it takes sap to harden into amber.)

- **Pages 11–12** *Why is the amber found today in pieces?* (Long ago, ocean waves broke amber into small and large pieces.)

- **Page 13** *What causes amber to look cloudy rather than clear?* (Air bubbles in the amber make it look cloudy.)

- **Pages 14–15** *Why do you think a scientist would be most interested in a piece of amber that held a plant, animal, or insect?* (The scientist can study the plant, animal, or insect trapped in the amber to find out more about life long ago.)

- **Page 16** *Why do you think amber is called "a golden trap"?* (The color of amber is like gold. The things a piece of amber can trap are as valuable as gold to a scientist who wants to study them.)

Reading Strategies

If... a student does not understand that amber began forming long, long ago,	**Then...** have him or her search the book for time references, such as "a very long time ago."
If... a student has difficulty distinguishing statements of fact and opinion,	**Then...** use **Model Your Thinking** below.

Model Your Thinking

Think ALOUD

Comprehension Skill: Fact and Opinion

A statement of fact tells something that can be proved true or false. A statement of opinion tells someone's ideas or feelings. Words such as *like, believe,* or *should* are clues that a statement is an opinion. This book is full of facts about amber. On page 3, the author writes, "People have worn amber for many years." I recognize that as a fact since I could check in an encyclopedia or ask a jewelry expert to prove whether that statement was true or false. On page 14, I see the word *like.* This statement expresses an opinion because it tells how scientists feel about amber filled with plants, animals, or insects. Good readers identify statements of fact or opinion because it helps them think about the author's ideas.

After Reading

Revisiting the Text

Comprehension Use the T-Chart on page 150. Write the heads *Fact* and *Opinion* at the top of the columns. Have pairs reread the book and identify three interesting statements of fact. Then have partners form one opinion about the book or its information.

69B

Basketball!

by Nat Gabriel
Leveled Reader 69B
Genre: Informational Article
Level: Easy/Average

Summary

What would you do with a roomful of bored schoolboys who needed entertaining? In 1891, a clever teacher nailed two fruit baskets to opposite walls and invented basketball. Over the years, the game has changed, but it's clear to see it all began with that one good idea.

At a Glance

Links to the Student Edition

Comprehension Skill: Fact and Opinion

Selection Vocabulary: *alert, breaks, melt*

Program Theme: The World Around Us
Unit Theme: The Whole Wide World

Throughout the whole wide world, people play games and sports. Basketball is an American sport that was invented to keep bored school boys entertained.

Before Reading

Motivating the Reader

Build Background about Basketball

Bring a basketball to class and show a videotape of basketball players in action. Invite students knowledgeable about the game to describe or demonstrate the basics of the game. Write terms such as *dribbling, passing, shooting, scoring, basket, hoop,* and *court* on the chalkboard. Have volunteers write definitions or draw pictures for each term. As students prepare to read the book, encourage them to compare what they know about basketball today to the game as it was played in 1891.

Preview and Predict

Have students scan the cover, text, and illustrations to get an idea of what the book is about. Ask them to compare and contrast the picture on the cover with the picture on pages 8–9. Help them use the pictures to predict the book's setting and topic. Suggest students read to find out how basketball was invented and how basketball has changed over the years.

Point out the selection vocabulary and any unfamiliar words, such as *bored, clever, inventing, dribbling,* and *grateful,* that might be important to understanding the book.

During Reading

Guiding Comprehension

Use the following questions to support students as they read.

- **Pages 2–3** *What words and picture clues tell you when the book is set?* ("It was 1891," and "a cold, winter day," tell when the book is set. The picture shows a lantern streetlight, snow, and an old brick schoolhouse. The boys in suits don't look like schoolchildren today.)

- **Pages 2–3** *How do the schoolboys feel? Why do they feel this way?* (They are bored and restless because the playground is covered with snow and ice and they can't play outside.)

- **Page 5** *What game do you think the teacher is inventing? How do you know?* (He is inventing *basketball*. The book title is *Basketball!* and I saw pictures of the schoolboys playing basketball while previewing.)

- **Page 6** *In the new game, what does a player try to do?* (The object is to throw a ball into a basket on the wall.)

- **Pages 9–10** *What new problem arises during the game?* (When a ball goes in the basket, players can't get it out.) *How does the teacher solve it?* (He uses a ladder to get the ball out.) *Do players today have this problem? Explain.* (No. Today a net with a hole in the bottom lets the ball fall through.)

- **Pages 14–15** *What are ways basketball today is like that first game? What are ways it is different?* (Similarities include shooting a ball in a basket, having a basket at each end of a space, and having two teams play. Differences include using a net instead of a basket, dribbling, passing, fast breaks, new rules, coaches, and uniforms.)

- **Page 16** *How does the author feel about the teacher who invented basketball?* (He thinks the teacher was creative. He thinks people should be grateful to the teacher for inventing the game.)

Model Your Thinking

 Comprehension Skill: Fact and Opinion

A statement of fact tells something that can be proved true or false. A statement of opinion tells someone's ideas or feelings. Words such as *like, believe,* or *should* are clues that a statement is an opinion. Page 6 states that the teacher used a soccer ball. That is a fact about the first type of ball used in basketball. I could prove this fact true or false by checking other sources of information about the invention of basketball. Also on page 6 the author gives his opinion, saying, "It was not as easy as it looked!". This is an opinion that shows what the author believes about the first basketball shot. It can't be proved true or false. As I read, I try to identify statements of fact and statements of opinion, so I can make decisions about what the author says.

After Reading

Revisiting the Text

Comprehension Have students reread the book and record statements of fact and opinion in the T-Chart on page 150. Have students take turns reading a statement from their chart. Other students should identify it as a fact or an opinion. Have students explain their reasoning.

70A
The River Rescue

by B.G. Hennessy
Leveled Reader 70A
Genre: Realistic Story
Level: Easy

Summary

Dad takes Rosa and Roberto to a quiet river for what he hopes will be a peaceful and enjoyable day. However, Rosa and Roberto soon add excitement to the day when their lunch floats down the river in their tubes and they get stranded on an island. All turns out well when Dad rescues his children, and the police return the missing food and tubes.

At a Glance

Links to the Student Edition

☞ **Comprehension Skill:** Main Idea and Supporting Details

Selection Vocabulary: *island, cardboard, cliff*

Program Theme: The World Around Us
Unit Theme: The Whole Wide World

A quiet and peaceful day exploring a river can turn into an adventure when unexpected events occur.

Before Reading

Motivating the Reader
Build Background About Rivers

Discuss with the students how they would describe a river to someone who has never seen one. If necessary, show pictures or a videotape of a river. Talk with students about what is fun about a river and what is dangerous. Then encourage them to draw a picture of what they would most enjoy doing if they were spending a day at the river.

Preview and Predict

Have students scan the cover, text, and the illustrations to get an idea of what the book is about. Have them use picture and word clues to make predictions about who will go to the river and what will happen at the river. Students can write a prediction about a problem they think the characters will face in the Story Prediction organizer on page 130. They can complete the organizer after reading the book. Suggest that students read to find out whether the children in the book do the same kinds of things as students drew in their river pictures.

Point out the selection vocabulary and any unfamiliar words, such as *rapids, navigator,* and *towing,* that might be important to understanding the book.

During Reading

Guiding Comprehension

Use the following questions to support students as they read.

- **Pages 2–3** Why is Saturday a special day for Rosa and Roberto? (Their dad is taking them to the river.)

- **Page 4** What do Rosa and Roberto hope they might find at the river? What does Dad tell them they will find? (Roberto hopes there will be rapids. Rosa hopes there will be sharks. Dad tells them there will be peace and quiet.)

- **Page 5** Look at what the family is taking with them to the river. What do you predict the family will do at the river? (Predictions should include activities that use the items shown, such as fishing with the fishing pole.)

- **Page 7** What does a navigator do? (A navigator tells how to get to a specific place.)

- **Page 12** What is an island? How do the children get to the island? (An island is land surrounded by water. The children float to the island on their tubes.)

- **Page 14** What happens to the children's lunch and the tubes? (The tubes float away. Their lunch was in a box that was on a tube.)

- **Page 14** What does the word *stranded* mean? Use context clues and the picture to figure out the meaning of the word. (It means "not being able to leave a place.")

- **Page 16** What were some of the children's adventures that day? (They almost got lost on the way to the river; they lost their tubes and lunches; they were stranded on the island.)

- **Page 16** How do Rosa, Roberto, and Dad feel about their time at the river? How do you know? (They enjoyed the day. All of them are smiling. Rosa and Roberto say it was great. Dad laughs about their adventures.)

Reading Strategies

If... a student has trouble understanding the word *rapids* on page 4,	**Then...** have the student use context clues as well as the illustrations to interpret what the word means.
If... a student cannot interpret the thought balloons on page 4,	**Then...** point out to her or him that thought balloons show what someone is thinking or imagining.
If... a student has difficulty identifying the book's main idea and supporting details,	**Then...** use **Model Your Thinking** below.

Model Your Thinking

 Comprehension Skill: Main Idea and Supporting Details

Think ALOUD

When I want to think about or tell someone else about a fictional story I've read, I ask myself, "What is this story all about?" As I skim through the book and look at its words and pictures, I can tell that it is all about a family's adventures at a river. Then I look for story details that support my answer. The family almost gets lost on the way to the river. Then the children lose their tubes and get stranded on an island. These details show what kind of adventures the family had at the river.

After Reading

Revisiting the Text

Comprehension Tell students that titles are often good clues to what a book is all about. Ask students if they think *The River Rescue* is a good title for this book. Have them reread the book and suggest new titles for it, giving reasons to support their suggestions. Students can then vote on the title they like best. They can work in groups to create new book covers to match the new title.

70B

Big and Small Homes for All

by Joanne Mattern
Leveled Reader 70B
Genre: Informational Article
Level: Easy/Average

Summary

Different birds build nests in many shapes and sizes to keep themselves and their families safe. They build them from all kinds of material they find nearby, such as grass, twigs, clay, rocks, paper, and even string.

At a Glance

Links to the Student Edition

◉ **Comprehension Skill:** Main Idea and Supporting Details

Selection Vocabulary: *hatch, searching, underground, burrows*

Program Theme: The World Around Us
Unit Theme: The Whole Wide World

As we explore the world of nature, we find many similarities among living things.

Before Reading

Motivating the Reader
Build Background About Shelters

Ask students how they might build their homes if they lived a long time ago in places such as a forest, a desert, in the Arctic, or on the Great Plains. Discuss students' ideas, and point out that people had to use whatever materials were nearby. If possible, provide pictures of dugouts, igloos, teepees, and other types of shelters. Then ask students to think about the different kinds of homes birds and other animals might build.

Preview and Predict

Have students scan the cover, text and illustrations to get an idea of what the book is about. After they have scanned the book, use the K-L-W Chart on page 135 to list their responses. Write in the first column what students know about their nests from their own experience and observation. In the second column, have them write questions about birds' nests that they predict the book will help them answer. Encourage students to look for answers to their questions as they read. They can complete their charts after they have read the book.

Point out the selection vocabulary and any unfamiliar words, such as *knotted, flamingo, tunnel, waterproof,* and *sawdust,* that might be important to understanding the book.

During Reading

Guiding Comprehension

Use the following questions to support students as they read.

- **Page 3** *Which words tell what size birds' nests are?* (big, small) *Which words tell where birds build their nests?* (high branches, underground burrow)

- **Page 3** *What is an underground burrow?* (It is a hole dug underground.)

- **Page 5** *What are these sentences all about?* (They tell about the different things birds use to build their nests.)

- **Page 6** *From what you've read so far, what do you think the rest of this book will be about?* (about how different birds build their nests)

- **Page 7** *What shape is a robin's nest?* (It is shaped like a bowl.) *How does a robin make her nest into this shape?* (She pushes her body into the pile of twigs she has stuck together with mud. She then twists and turns to get the twigs into a bowl shape.)

- **Pages 8–9** *How does the weaver bird build its nest?* (It makes a ring of grass, hangs the ring from a tree, and uses its beak to weave the grass around and around the ring.)

- **Pages 11–12** *How are ovenbirds, flamingos, and swallows all alike?* (They build their nests out of mud.)

- **Page 13** *Why do you think that the hornbill seals herself inside of a hole in a tree?* (She does it to protect herself and her eggs.)

- **Page 14** *Why might a swallow build its nest in a traffic light?* (The heat from the lights may keep the eggs warm.)

- **Page 15** *Why does a woodpecker build its nest inside of trees?* (Woodpeckers eat insects that live in trees. It builds its nest inside trees so it is close to the food it eats.)

- **Page 16** *Why does the writer call a nest a home?* (It is a safe place where birds live and raise their families just like people's homes.)

Reading Strategies

If...	Then...
If... a student cannot figure out what an underground burrow is,	**Then...** have the student break apart *underground* and picture a nest dug underground.
If... a student has difficulty understanding how a specific nest is made,	**Then...** tell the student to check the photograph carefully to see what additional information can be found there.
If... a student has difficulty identifying main ideas and supporting details,	**Then...** use **Model Your Thinking** below.

Model Your Thinking

Think ALOUD

 Comprehension Skill: Main Idea and Supporting Details

The main idea of a paragraph tells what the sentences are all about. It is the most important idea in a paragraph. Sometimes this is stated in the paragraph; sometimes you need to figure it out. Supporting details are smaller pieces of information that tell more about the main idea. For example, on page 5, all these sentences tell about the things birds use to build their nests. Each sentence is a supporting detail that tells more about this main idea. Finding the main idea of a paragraph and its supporting details helps me make sure I've understood what I've read and it helps me remember it too.

After Reading

Revisiting the Text

Comprehension Have students use the Main Idea organizer on page 142. Assign students different paragraphs or sections of the book to reread. Have students write the main idea in the single box at the top of the page. Then have them write supporting details in the boxes below. Students can draw additional boxes as needed.

71A
Cynthia Rylant

A Writer's Story

by Alice Cary
Leveled Reader 71A
Genre: Biography
Level: Easy

Summary

As author Cynthia Rylant grew up, she discovered an interest and talent in writing. This biography describes the experiences and interests in her life which inspire her to write. A quiet and private person, she finds satisfaction and courage through writing her books.

At a Glance

Links to the Student Edition

☞ **Comprehension Skill:** Steps in a Process

Selection Vocabulary: *authors, difficult, libraries, museums*

Program Theme: Learning and Working
Unit Theme: Getting the Job Done

Sitting quietly and thinking may not seem like work to everyone, but it is if you're a writer searching for just the right idea for a great story.

Before Reading

Motivating the Reader
Build Background About Writing

Invite students to share their experiences, good and bad, with trying to write something. Help students outline the writing process from getting an idea to publishing your work. Then brainstorm tips for each step in the process that would help someone learn how to be a good writer. Encourage students to compare their experiences writing with Cynthia Rylant's experiences as they read the book.

Preview and Predict

Have students scan the cover, text, and illustrations to get an idea of what the book is about. Draw students' attention to the book title and the genre label on the back cover. Discuss what they know about biographies. Help students make predictions about the book by asking:

> Who do you think Cynthia Rylant is? What does she do? What kinds of information do you think will be in this book?

Encourage students to read to find the answers to these questions.

Point out selection vocabulary and any unfamiliar words, such as *publisher, imagination, admired,* and *timid,* that might be important to understanding the book.

During Reading

Guiding Comprehension

Use the following questions to support students as they read.

- **Page 2** What does Cynthia Rylant *do for work?* (She is an author.)

- **Pages 3–4** What was Rylant's life like as a *child?* (She lived with her grandparents. She didn't have a lot of money. She didn't get to read very many books. She says she felt rich because she loved everything about life.)

- **Page 5** What did Rylant find that was new and interesting to her? (She found children's books.) Which sentence shows how much she loved children's books? ("She read them every night.")

- **Page 6** What does *admired* mean? Restate this sentence in your own words. (She liked the work the authors did very much.)

- **Page 7** What happened when Rylant was twenty-five years old? (She sent a book to a publisher, and they agreed to publish it.) What was the title of the first story she published? *(When I Was Young in the Mountains)*

- **Page 9** How does Rylant get some of her ideas for stories? (She watches for fun places, listens for funny names, and writes about things she loves.)

- **Page 10** Who are Mr. Putter, Mudge, and Zeke? (They are characters in stories that Cynthia Rylant has written.)

- **Page 13** How does Rylant begin writing? What word is a clue that this is the first step? (She starts with her imagination. *Starts* is a clue that this is the first step.)

- **Page 14** What do you think Rylant is waiting for? (She is waiting for ideas to come.)

- **Page 16** What opposite word on this page helps you understand the meaning of *timid?* (Brave is the opposite of *timid. Timid* means "not brave.")

Model Your Thinking

 Comprehension Skill: Steps in a Process

Steps in a process are the steps you follow to do or make something. As I read, I look for clue words such as *first* and *then* that tell the order of the steps. On page 12, I read about how Cynthia Rylant makes illustrations for her stories. I try to picture these steps in my head. It makes sense that she goes to the store first to get what she needs. The clue word *then* tells me that making the illustrations comes after she buys paper and scissors. The picture also helps me understand that after making her illustrations, she uses her scissors to cut them out. Thinking about these steps helps me better understand the work that Cynthia Rylant does.

After Reading

Revisiting the Text

Comprehension Use the Steps in a Process organizer on page 148. Have pairs reread pages 13–14 and list the steps Cynthia Rylant follows when writing, breaking "imagination" into the three steps described on page 14. Discuss each step with students, and encourage them to tell what happens once she finishes writing a book.

71B

Andy's Handy–Dandy Bubble–Band Beanie

by Sarah Weeks
Leveled Reader 71B
Genre: Humorous Story
Level: Easy/Average

Summary

Andy is an enthusiastic inventor with a problem. His inventions have already been invented! He is very discouraged, until his loving wife Mary notices the amazing hat he has made that blows bubbles and plays music. Andy and Mary work together to come up with a name for his clever invention and dance to celebrate Andy's success.

At a Glance

Links to the Student Edition

◉ **Comprehension Skill:** Steps in a Process

Selection Vocabulary: *information, suggestions*

Program Theme: Learning and Working
Unit Theme: Getting the Job Done

Ideas for great inventions aren't always easy to find. Sometimes it takes friends or family to point out what is right in front of you.

Before Reading

Motivating the Reader
Build Background About Inventions

If possible, show pictures of various common machines, such as a mixer, a washing machine, and a power saw. Invite pairs to act out a task without the help of the machine, such as mixing a cake with a spoon, washing clothes by hand, and cutting a huge log with a hand saw. One partner shows the task, and then the other partner plays the role of a salesman/inventor of a machine that will make the task easier. Encourage each pair to make up their own name for the "invention," explain how it works, and tell why it is helpful.

Preview and Predict

Have students scan the cover, text, and illustrations to get an idea of what the book is about. Point out the strange machines on the cover. Ask students to use these picture clues to tell who the man might be and what he might do for a living. Encourage students to make predictions about what events might happen in the book. Have them set their own purpose for reading, such as reading to find out what a Handy-Dandy Bubble-Band Beanie is.

Point out selection vocabulary and any unfamiliar words, such as *lab, handy-dandy, amazing,* and *beanie,* that might be important to understanding the book.

During Reading

Guiding Comprehension

Use the following questions to support students as they read.

- **Page 2** **What does Andy make in his lab?** (He makes inventions in his lab.)

- **Page 3** **What is the first step to make Andy's Handy-Dandy Bread Warmer work?** (You plug it in.) **What is the last step?** (The warm bread pops up.)

- **Page 4** **Mary says Andy's Bread Warmer has already been invented. What is it?** (It is a toaster.)

- **Page 4** **Why does Mary pat his arm?** (Answers will vary. She is trying to make him feel better because he is feeling sad and discouraged that his "invention" is not something new.)

- **Page 5** **What will Andy do next?** (He will go back to his lab to try to make another invention.)

- **Page 7** **Do you think Andy's Handy-Dandy Dirt Sucker works well? How do you know?** (It probably doesn't work well because there is smoke coming out of it. The picture shows it makes more of a mess than it cleans up. Mary's face looks upset.)

- **Page 9** **What does his wife always say to him when he goes back into his lab?** (She says, "Good luck, dear.") **Why does she say this?** (to encourage him about making another invention)

- **Page 11** **How does Andy feel? Why does he feel this way?** (He feels sad and discouraged because he can't think of anything to invent that isn't already invented.)

- **Pages 12–13** **What does Mary notice that is amazing?** (She notices Andy's hat.)

- **Page 14** **What does Andy's Hat do?** (It keeps his head warm, plays music, and blows bubbles.)

- **Page 16** **How does Andy feel now? Why did his feelings change?** (He feels better because he finally has an invention that no one else has already invented.)

Model Your Thinking

 Comprehension Skill: Steps in a Process

 Think ALOUD

Steps in a process are the steps you follow to do or make something. Good readers look for clue words like *first*, *next*, and *then* to figure out the order of the steps. They also try to picture the steps in their head to figure out an order that makes sense. For example, on page 3, Andy tells Mary how to work his Handy-Dandy Bread Warmer, by saying, "First plug it in. Next put in a slice of bread. Then push the button." These words *first*, *next*, and *then* help me figure out the order in which the steps happen. The next sentence, "Wait a bit.", does not have a clue word, but it makes sense that this step would come next since it would take a while for the bread to get warm. Thinking about these steps helps me better understand how Andy's invention works.

After Reading

Revisiting the Text

Comprehension Use the Steps in a Process organizer on page 148. Have pairs record the steps for using Andy's Handy-Dandy Bread Warmer. They can use prior knowledge, story details, and their imagination to make up steps for using Andy's other two inventions. Invite students to share their organizers.

72A
What Frank Watched

by Rosie Bensen
Leveled Reader 72A
Genre: Humorous Story
Level: Easy

Summary

After receiving a TV set as a gift, Frank tries to learn to like watching television. He tries to find something interesting or clever about it, but can't. Then Frank's friends explain that television is less dull if you turn the set on first. While Frank's friends share what they know about television, Frank shares his love of reading with them.

At a Glance

Links to the Student Edition

☞ **Comprehension Skill:** Summarizing

Selection Vocabulary: *clever, lazy, cheated, business, wealth*

Program Theme: Learning and Working
Unit Theme: Getting the Job Done

Sharing your knowledge and opinions can help you and your friends discover new things and have fun together.

Before Reading

Motivating the Reader
Build Background About Hobbies

Give students an outline of a simple bar graph with the days of the week across the horizontal axis and hours marked off on the vertical axis. Help students draw bars to show how much television they watch each day. Invite students to share their graphs. Then ask students to imagine what it would be like to spend an entire week without a television. Invite them to suggest hobbies or interests that they could share with their friends or family members instead of watching television. Discuss what they like about watching television and what they like about the other hobbies or interests they suggested. Encourage students to think about what the main character likes to do besides watching television as they read the book.

Preview and Predict

Have students scan the cover, text, and illustrations to get an idea of what the book is about. Ask them to look for details in the illustrations that help them figure out who Frank is and what sorts of things he likes to do. Draw their attention to the book's title set inside a television set. Ask them to predict what it is that Frank will watch and what problem this story will tell about. Suggest they read to find out how the problem is solved.

Point out selection vocabulary and any unfamiliar words, such as *repair, interesting,* and *mystery,* that might be important to understanding the book.

During Reading

Guiding Comprehension

Use the following questions to support students as they read.

- **Page 2** **What did Steve give Frank?** (He gave him a television set.)

- **Page 3** **What do Frank's friends and brother think about the gift?** (They like it. They think Frank will enjoy watching good shows on television.) **How do you think Frank feels about the gift? How do you know?** (He seems a bit puzzled by the gift. He has never owned a TV and he is scratching his head as he looks at it.)

- **Page 3** **What does wealth mean? Can you restate Steve's statement in your own words?** (It means "to have a lot of something." There are many good shows on television.)

- **Page 3** Look at Frank's house. **What do you think Frank likes to do? Why?** (Because he has so many books, Frank probably loves to read.)

- **Page 4** **What happens when Frank watches television?** (He doesn't see anything interesting.)

- **Page 6** **Why didn't Frank find anything clever to watch?** (He doesn't have the television set turned on.)

- **Pages 6–8** **Why did Frank keep watching television?** (He was sure that he would see something amazing. All his friends liked it, so he thought he would like it too.)

- **Page 9** **What kind of program will Frank watch next?** (a mystery) **What do you think will happen next?** (He won't see anything on the television because he hasn't turned it on.)

- **Page 13** **Why does Frank say, "Oops!"?** (He realizes that there was nothing on television because he did not turn it on.)

- **Page 14** **Where does Frank know there is a good mystery?** (in a book)

- **Page 16** **What did Frank and his friends enjoy doing together?** (They enjoyed reading good mystery books.)

Model Your Thinking

Comprehension Skill: Summarizing

Authors often give you a lot of information. As they read, good readers need to decide which information is the most important. Summarizing means telling about the most important ideas or events in a book in just a few sentences. To summarize this book, I might say: Frank got a television set from his brother. However, every time Frank tried to watch television, there was nothing interesting on television. Then Frank discovered that he needed to turn the television set on first! While Frank's friends taught him about television, he shared his knowledge of good books with them. Summarizing stories like this is a good way to help me remember what I've read.

After Reading

Revisiting the Text

Comprehension Invite pairs to write a short book review. Explain that a book review includes a short summary of the book and tells what the reader liked or didn't like about it. Students can use the Plot/Story Sequence organizer on page 137 to tell what happens in the book and then decide which events are the most important.

72B
From Top to Bottom

Carving a Totem Pole

by Diane Hoyt-Goldsmith
Leveled Reader 72B
Genre: Realistic Story
Level: Easy/Average

Summary

George and his father are carving a totem pole. When George tries to carve like his father, he realizes that carving is more difficult than it looks. George is frustrated because he isn't as good as his father, but his father assures him that he will get better. George is happy knowing that someday he'll be a great carver like his father.

At a Glance

Links to the Student Edition

 Comprehension Skill: Summarizing

Selection Vocabulary: *partners, harvesting*

Program Theme: Learning and Working
Unit Theme: Getting the Job Done

Learning a new skill can be both frustrating and rewarding. If you keep trying, you will become better and better and learn to do the job well.

Before Reading

Motivating the Reader
Build Background About Learning New Skills

Invite students to share their experiences about learning how to do something new, like building something, riding a bike, painting, or cooking. Ask them if they made mistakes and how they learned to do the skill well. Tell the students to imagine they have a friend who feels bad because he makes mistakes while working on a project with his father. Ask students to think about what advice they would give their friend. Have pairs write a letter to their friend to help him with his problem.

Preview and Predict

Have students scan the cover, text, and illustrations to get an idea of what the book is about. Draw their attention to the book title and ask students what they know about totem poles and what they think they might learn from reading the story. Have students identify the two main characters and make predictions about what will happen to these characters. Suggest they read to find out if their predictions are correct.

Point out selection vocabulary and any unfamiliar words, such as *gravel, sketched,* and *clumsy,* that might be important to understanding the book.

During Reading

Guiding Comprehension

Use the following questions to support students as they read.

- **Pages 2–3** *Who are the two characters that are in the story?* (George and his father) *What are they doing?* (They are driving to the place where they will carve a totem pole.)

- **Pages 4–5** *What is a totem pole?* (It is a tall pole made from a cedar log with carvings on it.)

- **Pages 6–7** *What figures will George and his father carve in the totem pole?* (They will carve a raven, a bear, and a killer whale.)

- **Page 8** *What did George do on this page to help his father?* (He brought him the knife.)

- **Pages 8–9** *Why do you think George and his father are wearing special glasses?* (The glasses will protect their eyes from any wood chips.)

- **Page 9** *What happens when George tries to carve with the knife?* (He makes rough and jagged cuts.) *Why did his father tell him not to worry?* (Answers will vary. His father knows making mistakes is part of learning.)

- **Page 11** *What happens when George tries to use the adz?* (He can't get it to cut the wood.)

- **Pages 12–13** *What step happens after the carving is finished?* (The totem pole is painted.) *What happens during this step?* (George knocks over the paint cans.)

- **Pages 14–15** *How does George feel when he first sees the finished totem pole? Why does he feel this way?* (He feels unimportant and upset because he made so many mistakes.)

- **Page 16** *How does George feel at the end of the story? Why did his feelings change?* (He feels better because his dad tells him that, each time they carve, George will get better.)

Reading Strategies

If... a student doesn't understand what an adz is,	**Then...** have the student reread the text and tell how it is used.
If... a student has difficulty understanding that George's feelings change,	**Then...** point to the words *frowned* and *smiled* on pages 15 and 16 and ask the student to tell what these actions mean.
If... a student has difficulty summarizing,	**Then...** use **Model Your Thinking** below.

Model Your Thinking

🎯 **Comprehension Skill: Summarizing**

Think ALOUD

When you summarize a story, you tell in a few short sentences what happens in the story. A good summary includes just the most important events in the story; it doesn't include all the less important details. To summarize this story, I would say: George and his father are carving a totem pole together. When George tries to carve like his father, he makes some mistakes. When George gets upset about these mistakes, his father explains that, each time they carve, George will get better and someday George will be a carver like him. Note that I didn't tell about each mistake George made. These details are less important, so I left them out. Summarizing is a good way to help me remember what I've read.

After Reading

Revisiting the Text

Comprehension Have groups reread the book and use the Story Sequence organizer on page 139 to describe what happens in the story. Then have them create a book jacket cover with a blurb that summarizes the story. Remind students to include only the most important events in their summaries.

73A
Class Clowns

by Meish Goldish
Leveled Reader 73A
Genre: Informational Article
Level: Easy

Summary

Do you think it's all fun and games being a clown? This book tells about a special school where people go to learn how to be a clown. There are many skills to master, as well as having fun. It takes hard work and lots of practice to learn to make people laugh.

At a Glance

Links to the Student Edition

☞ **Comprehension Skill:** Text Structure

Selection Vocabulary: *direction, guide, introduce, patient, harness*

Program Theme: Learning and Working
Unit Theme: Getting the Job Done

Even a job which helps people laugh takes time and practice to learn. Schools are a place where you can learn to do things well.

Before Reading

Motivating the Reader
Build Background About Clowns

Ask students to think of places and events where they have seen clowns and the kinds of things clowns do to make people laugh. Have students draw pictures of a clown doing a trick, such as juggling, riding a unicycle, walking on stilts, or moving their bodies in funny ways. Invite students to tell about their pictures. Discuss whether these tricks would be easy or difficult to learn and what steps are involved in learning these tricks.

Preview and Predict

Have students scan the cover, text, and illustrations to get an idea of what the book is about. Prepare students to read by drawing their attention to the book's cover and ask:

> What are class clowns? Do you think these words have more than one meaning? Who are these people? What do you think they do? This sign above the door says "Clown College." What might you learn at a clown college?

Discuss students' predictions and encourage them to read to find out if their predictions are correct.

Point out selection vocabulary, unfamiliar words, and slang phrases, such as *clown around, get my act together,* or *ups and downs.*

During Reading

Guiding Comprehension

Use the following questions to support students as they read.

- **Page 2** Look at the picture and read this page. Who is telling or narrating the story? (The clown in the front of the picture with the pie in her face is telling the story.)

- **Page 3** What did the narrator of the story do to become a clown? (She took classes at a special school.)

- **Page 4** Why does the narrator say it isn't easy to get into clown school? (A lot of people want to go to school, but there isn't enough room to accept everyone.)

- **Page 4** What is an audition? (It is a try out when people perform with the hope that they will be chosen to go to the clown school.)

- **Page 5** What does it mean to "clown around"? (It means "to act silly.") Why can you clown around at clown school? (You are supposed to act silly when you're learning to be a clown.)

- **Pages 6–9** What kinds of skills are taught at clown school? (walking on stilts, riding a unicycle, walking on a high wire, juggling rings)

- **Page 10** What types of things do students do at clown school to keep in shape? (They run around, fall down, and roll over.)

- **Page 11** Why might a raincoat be helpful when you are learning to be a clown? (A raincoat will keep you dry while you learn how to shoot and spit water.)

- **Page 13** How do they want you to dress at clown school? (They want you to look silly.)

- **Page 15** What did the narrator do for her special trick? (She juggled while riding a unicycle on a high wire.)

- **Page 16** What does the narrator do for a job now? (She works as a clown in a circus.)

- **Page 16** How is information in this book organized? (The narrator tells in order what she learned in clown school.)

Reading Strategies

If... the student is unsure of the gender of the narrator,	**Then...** point out that the same girl appears in all the pictures on pages 6–9.
If... a student has trouble explaining how the text is organized,	**Then...** use **Model Your Thinking** below.

Model Your Thinking

🎯 **Comprehension Skill: Text Structure**

Think ALOUD

Text structure is the way a piece of writing is organized. Because Class Clowns tells facts about a real clown and clown school, I know it is a nonfiction book. Writers may organize information in a nonfiction book in different ways. While I read, I look to see how the information about clown school is organized. On page 4, I learn about how you get into a clown school. Pages 6–11 are about what a clown learns in clown school. Each page tells about something different. At the end, the narrator graduates and now works in a circus. This book is like a journey from the start to the finish of clown school. Thinking about the text structure helps me better understand and remember what I've read.

After Reading

Revisiting the Text

Comprehension Use Web 1 on page 132. Have pairs reread the book and use the web to record details or sketch pictures about what is taught in clown school. Have pairs share their webs. Discuss how information in the book is organized. Have students tell which part of clown school would be their favorite and why.

73B
A Pig Mystery

by Fay Robinson
Leveled Reader 73B
Genre: Animal Fantasy
Level: Easy/Average

Summary

When a very messy pig hears scary scratching noises and finds some of his food is missing and his newspapers shredded, he seeks help from the police and a detective. Both of them tell him to clean up his sty. The pig isn't interested in changing his ways, until he discovers gophers have made his mess their new home.

At a Glance

Links to the Student Edition

Comprehension Skill: Text Structure

Selection Vocabulary: *bounded, easily, correcting*

Program Theme: Learning and Working
Unit Theme: Getting the Job Done

Keeping your things neat and clean may be work, but it can solve some very messy problems.

Before Reading

Motivating the Reader
Build Background About Animal Characters

Invite students to share some of their favorite make-believe stories where animals can talk and do other amazing things. Have them describe the characters and tell what they do. Make a list on the chalkboard sorting the characters by animal type. Discuss the character traits that are often associated with a particular type of animal, such as a clever fox, a slow turtle, or a messy pig. Have students draw pictures of their favorite kind of animal character and describe what character traits they associate with this animal.

Preview and Predict

Have students scan the cover, text, and illustrations. Draw their attention to the book title, and discuss what usually happens in a mystery. Prepare students to read by asking:

> Who are the characters in this book? Look at how they are dressed and how they act. What do you think these characters are like? What do you think they will do in this book?

Encourage students to check their predictions as they read, changing them as needed as they read new information.

Point out selection vocabulary and any unfamiliar words, such as *attacked, burrow, shrugged,* and *sty,* that might be important to understanding the book.

During Reading

Guiding Comprehension

Use the following questions to support students as they read.

- **Pages 2–3** **What is the pig's home like?** (It is very messy. Food and clothing are everywhere.)

- **Pages 2–3** **What happened to make the pig turn down his TV?** (He heard an odd sound.)

- **Page 4** **Why can't the pig sleep?** (He hears more noises. He is afraid someone or something might attack him.)

- **Page 5** **Why did he call the police?** (Someone stole his vegetables.)

- **Pages 6–7** **Why is Sergeant Smith in a hurry to leave? What picture clues help you figure this out?** (The pig's sty is smelly. The police officer is holding his nose. The wavy lines near the dirt pile show that it smells.)

- **Page 7** **What is a sty?** (It is the place where a pig lives.)

- **Pages 8–9** **Why does the pig save the newspaper almost every day?** (The newspapers often have stories about his brother, the mayor.) **Who do you think might have shredded the newspapers?** (Answers will vary. Some students may notice the furry face hidden on page 8.)

- **Page 12** **How does Detective Jones plan to solve the mystery?** (He will watch the pig while the pig watches TV and eats.)

- **Page 14** **What kind of animal does Detective Jones find in the hole?** (He finds a gopher.)

- **Pages 14–15** **What does the pig need to do to get rid of the gophers?** (He needs to clean up his sty.)

- **Page 16** **How did the pig change at the end of the book?** (He has become neat.)

- **Page 16** **How is information in this book organized?** (It begins with a mystery to be solved, clues are given, and then the mystery is solved.)

Model Your Thinking

 Comprehension Skill: Text Structure

 Think ALOUD

Text structure is the way a text is organized. Fiction tells stories about imaginary characters and events. It is usually organized to tell about events in the order that they happen. Since I know animals can't talk, I know that A *Pig Mystery* is fiction. Because it is also a mystery story, it is organized like other mysteries I've read. In the beginning there is a problem that needs to be solved, clues are given in the middle, and the mystery is solved at the end. Thinking about the text structure helps me follow what is happening in the story and remember it later.

After Reading

Revisiting the Text

Comprehension Have pairs reread the book and complete the Story Sequence organizer on page 139, by describing the events in the order that they are presented in the book. Then have pairs retell the story from another character's point of view, such as the gopher or Detective Jones. Remind the students to keep the order of events the same but to think about how they could be described through the eyes of the character.

74A
The New Kid

by Kari James
Leveled Reader 74A
Genre: Realistic Story
Level: Easy

Summary

Moving to a new neighborhood and going to a new school can be scary. The narrator's dad says that to make a friend you have to be a friend. To her surprise, her dad is right. She teaches Janet how to skateboard, and Janet helps her study for a spelling bee. By listening to her father's advice, she makes a friend and feels good about herself.

At a Glance

Links to the Student Edition

⌖ **Comprehension Skill:** Visualizing

Selection Vocabulary: *brave, afraid, spelling, reservation*

Program Theme: Learning and Working
Unit Theme: Getting the Job Done

By asking for help and sharing what you know, you can help yourself and others do a job well and make a friend in the process.

Before Reading

Motivating the Reader
Build Background About Making Friends

Ask students to suppose that they were in a new school and neighborhood. Encourage students who have had this experience to tell the thoughts and feelings they had when they first moved and what they did to make new friends. Encourage other students to discuss ways they could help a new student feel comfortable and welcome in their new school. Organize students into two groups. Have one group write a list of tips for how a new student can make friends. Have the other group write tips for making a new student feel welcomed.

Preview and Predict

Have students scan the cover, text, and illustrations to get an idea of what the book is about. Ask students to identify who the new kid is and how this character may be feeling. Ask students to make predictions about what problem this character may have and how it might be solved. Students can write their predictions in the Story Prediction organizer on page 130. They can complete the organizer after reading the book. Students can set their own purpose for reading, such as reading to find out what it is like to be the new kid in school.

Point out selection vocabulary and any unfamiliar words, such as *neighborhood, spelling bee,* and *decide,* that might be important to understanding the book.

During Reading

Guiding Comprehension

Use the following questions to support students as they read.

- **Page 3** Why does the narrator feel afraid? (She has just moved and doesn't have any friends yet.)

- **Pages 4–5** Why do you think the author repeats the words *new* and *different?* (The repetition shows just how strange everything seems to the girl, almost like a new world.)

- **Pages 6–7** How do the pictures help you understand why the narrator feels lonely? (The pictures show the girl doing things by herself while the other students do things together.)

- **Page 7** What do you think her father means? (He means that if you try being friendly toward someone then that person might become your friend.)

- **Page 11** What is the narrator going to ask Janet? Do you think talking to Janet is an easy or difficult thing to do? Why? (She is going to ask Janet to study spelling words with her. It is difficult to talk to someone you don't know because that person may not like you or want to talk with you.)

- **Page 13** How does Janet react to the narrator's idea? (She likes it. She wants to learn how to ride a skateboard.)

- **Page 13** How does the narrator feel now? (She feels better and a little more brave.) Why does she feel this way? (She is pleased that Janet wanted to spend time with her. She is glad she talked to Janet even if it was scary.)

- **Page 16** How does the narrator's feelings change by the end of the book? What has happened to change her feelings? (The narrator now feels happy because she has made a friend and doesn't feel so lonely.)

Reading Strategies

If... a student has trouble explaining how the narrator's feelings have changed,	Then... have the student compare the pictures on pages 2–11 with those on pages 12–16.
If... a student has difficulty visualizing,	Then... use **Model Your Thinking** below.

Model Your Thinking

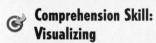 **Comprehension Skill: Visualizing**

Think ALOUD

Visualizing means picturing in your head what is happening in a story. Good readers try to picture how something looks, sounds, feels, tastes, or smells. To help me visualize, I look at the words an author uses to describe characters, places, and events. I also think about what I already know about people, places, and events that are like the ones I read about in the story. For example, on page 5, the narrator says that her new school "looks different. It feels different. And it even smells different." After I read the page, I close my eyes for a minute and imagine I am in a new school. I imagine how it looks, how it feels, and how it smells. Visualizing this place helps me better understand what the narrator is feeling.

After Reading

Revisiting the Text

Comprehension Ask students to reread pages 4–5 and visualize what the narrator sees, hears, tastes, touches, and smells on her first day in a new school. They can record their ideas in the Five-Column Chart on page 153. Then have students return to the Story Prediction organizers they began before reading, drawing a picture that shows the narrator's problem. Challenge students to include details in their drawings that aren't in the book's illustrations.

74B

How Coyote Gave Fire to People

retold by Maggie Bridger
Leveled Reader 74B
Genre: Folk Tale
Level: Easy/Average

Summary

Long ago, when the world was new, people were cold because they had no fur like the animals. To help the people, Coyote finds a way to trick the fireflies and steal some of their fire. The fireflies chase Coyote, so he gives the fire to the trees who swallow it up. From that day, people have been able to get fire from trees by rubbing sticks together.

At a Glance

Links to the Student Edition

Comprehension Skill: Visualizing

Selection Vocabulary: *silent, troubled*

Program Theme: Learning and Working
Unit Theme: Getting the Job Done
Patience and cleverness can help you get a difficult job done.

Before Reading

Motivating the Reader
Build Background About Fire

Ask students what they would do if they were very cold. Have them imagine what they would do if they were inside a house and what they would do if they were camping outside. Have students work in small groups to role-play a solution to this problem. Prompt students, if necessary, to act out a scene of building a campfire to stay warm when outside. Discuss ways that fire can be helpful to people.

Preview and Predict

Have students scan the cover, text, and illustrations to get an idea of what the book is about. Encourage students to tell what they know about folk tales. If needed, explain that folk tales often tell stories that help explain how things first happened in the world. The coyote is a common character in many Native American folk tales who often plays tricks on other characters. Ask students to make predictions about what this folk tale might explain about the world and what events might happen in the book. Suggest students read to find out how Coyote gave fire to people.

Point out selection vocabulary and any unfamiliar words, such as *shivered, loped,* and *guarded,* that might be important to understanding the book.

During Reading

Guiding Comprehension

Use the following questions to support students as they read.

- **Page 2** **When does this story take place?** (long ago when the world was new)

- **Page 3** **Why were the people silent?** (They were too cold to answer the animals.)

- **Pages 4–5** **Who has fire?** (the fireflies) **How does Mountain Lion try to get some fire?** (He asks the fireflies for it.) **What happens when Mountain Lion tries to get the fire?** (The fireflies laugh at Mountain Lion.)

- **Page 6** **What is another word that means almost the same as troubled?** (worried, concerned)

- **Pages 6–7** **How does Raven try to get fire?** (He tries to snatch it away from the fireflies.) **What happens next?** (The fireflies chase him away.)

- **Page 9** **What do you think Coyote will do with the drum?** (Answers will vary.)

- **Page 9** **What does loped mean?** (It tells how Coyote moves.)

- **Page 11** **When Coyote beat his drum, what did the fireflies do?** (They began to dance, and they forgot about the fire.)

- **Page 12** **What did Coyote use to get the fire?** (He used his tail.)

- **Page 14** **What did Coyote do with the fire?** (He passed it off to the trees.) **What did the trees do with the fire?** (They swallowed it.)

- **Page 15** **Why did the fireflies fly back to their meadow?** (They thought the lake had put Coyote's fire out.)

- **Page 16** **How does the story end?** (Coyote shows people how to make fire by rubbing sticks together.)

Reading Strategies

If... a student doesn't understand how the trees swallow the fire,	**Then...** remind the student that folk tales often describe incredible events that couldn't really happen.
If... a student has difficulty visualizing,	**Then...** use **Model Your Thinking** below.

Model Your Thinking

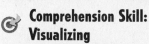 **Comprehension Skill: Visualizing**

Think ALOUD

Visualizing means creating pictures in your head of what is happening in a story. Good readers look for words an author uses to describe how things look, smell, taste, how they feel, or what sounds they make. It also helps to think about what you already know about what is being described. For instance, on page 11, I read about how Coyote beat his drum and how the fireflies danced. I try to imagine what the drum sounds like, what the burning fire smells like, how warm the fire feels, and what fireflies might look like dancing. Creating these pictures in my mind helps me better understand how Coyote tricks them. If you have a hard time creating a picture in your mind, reread the words again or read more slowly to get a better picture.

After Reading

Revisiting the Text

Comprehension Ask students to choose a favorite event from the book. Encourage them to read this part slowly and visualize what is happening. Have students use the Five-Column Chart on page 153 to record details related to their five senses. Invite students to share their mental images and their charts with others.

75A
Police Horse

by Susan McCloskey
Leveled Reader 75A
Genre: Informational Article
Level: Easy

Summary

Officer Lisa and her police horse Spree have a job that is both serious and fun. By going to a special school, Spree has learned what it takes to be a good police horse. Readers learn about how the two partners work together to help keep Portland, Maine, safe.

At a Glance

Links to the Student Edition

⌖ **Comprehension Skill:** Generalizing

Selection Vocabulary: *problem, serious, neighborhood, prove*

Program Theme: Learning and Working
Unit Theme: Getting the Job Done

Teamwork between a horse and a police officer helps keep people safe.

Before Reading

Motivating the Reader
Build Background About Teamwork

Ask students to imagine that they are a farmer trying to clear a field of heavy rocks. They are moving the rocks to the side of the field and using them to build a stone wall. Ask students to close their eyes and imagine themselves doing this task alone, without the help of any people, animals, or machines. Now ask them to imagine themselves doing this same task with the help of a horse and cart, and then also with the help of a few friends. Discuss how teamwork with animals or with other people helps them get the job done quicker and easier. Encourage students to think about how a horse and a police officer can work together as a team.

Preview and Predict

Have students scan the cover, text, and photographs to get an idea of what the book is about. Read the title aloud and ask students if they have ever seen a police horse. Invite them to discuss what they already know about police horses. Encourage them to make predictions about what a police horse does during a work day. Remind them to check and correct their predictions as they read.

Point out selection vocabulary and any unfamiliar words, such as *uniform, shoplifter,* and *steady,* that might be important to understanding the book.

During Reading

Guiding Comprehension

Use the following questions to support students as they read.

- **Page 2** **Who are the two partners in the book?** (a horse named Spree and Officer Lisa Sweat) **What job do these partners have?** (They work for the police department in Portland, Maine.)

- **Page 3** **Why does it take Officer Lisa and Spree two hours to get ready for work.** (Officer Lisa has to clean, feed, and saddle Spree and clean Spree's stall. Then she has to get into her uniform.)

- **Page 4** **What does this first sentence mean?** (It means that people will notice Spree and Officer Lisa in a crowd of people.)

- **Page 5** **What could Officer Lisa and Spree do that a police car couldn't?** (They could chase a shoplifter down a street where a police car couldn't travel.)

- **Page 6** **What happened to Spree and Officer Lisa that shows you their job can be dangerous?** (They were once hit by a car.)

- **Page 9** **What do you think "body language" is? Give an example.** (It is a way of communicating, or talking, using body movements instead of words. For example, if Spree rears up, he might be telling Officer Lisa that he sees a problem or he is scared.)

- **Page 10** **What part of Spree's job is fun?** (He gets to make friends with people.)

- **Page 12** **How do you think Spree and Kookie act when they are together?** (Answers will vary. They are playful; they may not listen to the officers as well.)

- **Page 15** **What happens in the winter?** (Spree has time off. Officer Lisa uses a police car instead of a horse.) **What makes it hard for Spree to work in the winter?** (Snow and ice make the streets slippery.)

Reading Strategies

If... a student has difficulty understanding why Spree takes a vacation in the winter,	**Then...** ask the student to think about what would happen if Spree tried to gallop on icy streets.
If... a student cannot identify generalizations or make generalizations,	**Then...** use **Model Your Thinking** below.

Model Your Thinking

 Comprehension Skill: Generalizing

 Think ALOUD

Generalizations are statements that tell how things or people are mostly alike in some way. Clue words like *sometimes, always, never, many,* or *all* signal generalizations. For example, pages 12 and 13 give generalizations about how Officer Lisa and Spree's workdays are alike. Sometimes they work with Kookie and another officer. Sometimes they work at night. After reading about Spree and Officer Lisa, I can make my own generalizations about police horses and police officers. For example I could say: *Police horses and police officers always work hard to keep our streets safe.*

After Reading

Revisiting the Text

Comprehension Review the book with students and help them identify generalizations about the work Spree and Officer Lisa do. Students can record these generalizations in Web 1 on page 132. Then encourage students to make generalizations that are based on the book, such as: *All police horses are well trained.* Invite students to share and discuss their generalizations.

75B
Believe Me

by Kana Riley
Leveled Reader 75B
Genre: Tall Tale
Level: Easy/Average

Summary

Augustus P. Frogbelly tells how he won a large prize trophy. Augustus needed to make a hole in one to win a golf tournament. It takes a twister, a circus tent, a duck, and a hot-air balloon to help him do it. Could this tale be true? While Augustus leaves it to readers to decide, the engraving on his trophy—Tall Tale Champ—makes one wonder.

At a Glance

Links to the Student Edition

Comprehension Skill: Generalizing

Selection Vocabulary: *prize, problem, jokes*

Program Theme: Learning and Working
Unit Theme: Getting the Job Done

You never know what help you may find when you are trying to accomplish something. This tall tale shows that help can sometimes come from unusual sources!

Before Reading

Motivating the Reader
Build Background About Golf

Draw a large word web on the chalkboard and write the word *golf* in the center. Ask students to brainstorm terms they associate with this sport, such as *club, tee, green, lead, hole in one*, and so on. Invite students who are knowledgeable about the game to explain what these terms mean and some basic rules for how the game is played and scored. Be sure students understand that the fewer strokes it takes to get the ball in the hole, the better the player's score will be. Ask students how likely it is to hit a hole in one.

Preview and Predict

Have students scan the cover, text, and illustrations to get an idea of what the book is about. Have students use word and picture clues to make predictions about what will happen in the story. Then ask them to predict whether this story will be a sad story or funny story and have them explain why they think so. Suggest students set their own purpose for reading, such as reading to find out what the book title means.

Point out selection vocabulary and any unfamiliar words, such as *trophy, tournament, compete, lead, hole in one, tee*, and *green*, that might be important to understanding the book.

During Reading

Guiding Comprehension

Use the following questions to support students as they read.

- **Page 2** **Who is telling the story?** (The frog, Augustus P. Frogbelly, is telling the story.)

- **Page 3** **What is his story going to be about?** (It will be about how Augustus won the prize trophy on his shelf.)

- **Page 4** **In what kind of contest is Augustus competing?** (He is competing in the Pebble Pond Golf Tournament.)

- **Page 5** **What does Augustus need to do to win the tournament?** (He needs a hole in one.)

- **Page 7** **What problem is described on this page?** (A twister scoops Augustus's ball out of the air.)

- **Pages 8–9** **Then what happens to the ball?** (The twister drops it on a circus tent. It bounces into the air and is caught by a duck who flies off with it.)

- **Page 9** **Why is the duck wearing a sign?** (It's a joke. The duck is carrying some small birds on her back and the sign makes it seem like she is an airplane with passengers.)

- **Page 11** **What happens to the balloon?** (The balloon springs a leak when the duck hits it and begins to go down toward the ground.)

- **Pages 12–14** **How does Augustus save the balloon passenger?** (Augustus has the passenger throw him a rope, and he pulls the rope so the balloon lands in the pond.)

- **Page 15** **What does the judge decide?** (He decides that Augustus's shot was a hole in one and that Augustus won the prize.)

- **Page 16** **Do you believe Augustus's story? Why or why not?** (Based on the engraving on the trophy and the incredible events, students should recognize that Augustus's story is a tall tale and isn't true.)

Reading Strategies

If... a student misses the significance of the trophy engraving,	Then... ask the student to explain what a tall tale champ would do to win a prize trophy.
If... a student cannot identify generalizations or make generalizations,	Then... use **Model Your Thinking** below.

Model Your Thinking

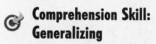 **Comprehension Skill: Generalizing**

 Think ALOUD

A statement that tells how several things or people are mostly alike is a generalization. Clue words like *sometimes, always, never, many,* or *all* signal generalizations. For example, on page 5, I read: "Not many people can get the ball into the hole in one swing." *Not many* tells me that most people can't get a hole in one. This generalization helps me understand how difficult it will be for Augustus to get a hole in one. I can also make my own generalizations about what I've read. For example, when I look at the writing on Augustus's trophy, I realize he has been telling me a tall tale. Based on what I've read in this book and what I've read in stories like this one, I can make the generalization that most tall tales stretch the truth in funny ways.

After Reading

Revisiting the Text

Comprehension Write the following generalization on the chalkboard: *Tall tales include exaggerations.* Have pairs reread the book to find examples from the book that support this generalization. Work with students to make other generalizations based on the book.

76A
Raven and Loon
An Inuit Tale

retold by Caren B. Stelson
Leveled Reader 76A
Genre: Folk Tale
Level: Easy

Summary

An Inuit child listens to his father tell a tale of how two friends, Raven and Loon, try to help each other become more beautiful. Tempers flare, and a disaster happens. While the tale gives an explanation of the colors and markings of a Raven and Loon, it also shows what can happen to friends after a misunderstanding.

Links to the Student Edition

ⓒ **Comprehension Skill:** Theme

Selection Vocabulary: *guest, stomach*

Program Theme: Traditions
Unit Theme: From Past to Present

An event which happened long ago changes two friends' appearances and their relationship.

Before Reading

Motivating the Reader
Build Background About Sharing

Ask for two volunteers to role-play. Place two chairs and other props which suggest two students working on an art project together. Ask one player to suppose that he or she has just spilled something on the other player's artwork. Ask students to role-play several reactions to this scene. Encourage students to discuss the characters' dilemma and possible solutions to this problem.

Preview and Predict

Have students scan the cover, text, and illustrations to get an idea of what the book is about. Encourage students to make predictions about the characters' personalities and what might happen in the book. Students can set their own purposes for reading, such as finding out what happens to the friendship between Raven and Loon.

Point out selection vocabulary and any unfamiliar words, such as *glaciers, dull,* and *glared,* that might be important to understanding the book.

During Reading

Guiding Comprehension

Use the following questions to support students as they read.

- **Page 2** What is happening on this page? (A father begins to tell a bedtime story.)

- **Pages 4–5** Why did Raven want to paint black spots on Loon? (Raven thought Loon's feathers looked dull.)

- **Page 7** How did Loon feel about the way he looked after Raven finished? What words tell you this? (He was pleased. It says, "he smiled to himself.")

- **Page 8** How did Raven feel about getting spots? (He wasn't sure he wanted them. He didn't think his gray feathers were dull.)

- **Pages 9–10** Why couldn't Raven hold still when Loon rubbed him with oil? (Loon rubbed too hard.)

- **Pages 10–11** Why did Raven break the stick in two? (He didn't want Loon to paint his feathers anymore, so he broke the stick Loon was using for painting.) **What did Loon do to Raven?** (He poured black oil all over Raven.)

- **Page 11** Do you agree with the narrator that Loon should not have poured the oil on Raven? Why or why not? (Yes. Even if Raven shouldn't have broken the painting stick, Loon's actions were mean.)

- **Pages 12–13** What did Raven do to Loon? (He hit Loon with the pot of oil.)

- **Page 13** How do Loon and Raven feel about each other at the end? How do you know? (They are no longer friends. They are both angry. Loon leaves Raven's house forever.)

- **Page 15** Folk tales often explain something about the world. What does this folk tale explain? (It explains how ravens got their shiny, black feathers and why loons move so awkwardly on land.)

- **Page 15** What lesson can you learn from this story? (Possible answer: Losing your temper can lead to disaster.)

Reading Strategies

If... a student stumbles over decoding the word *glaciers* on page 3,	Then... ask him or her to think about the two sounds the letter *c* can represent.
If... a student has difficulty identifying who is telling the story,	Then... ask him or her to reread page 2 and page 15 to find clues.
If... a student has trouble identifying the book's theme,	Then... use **Model Your Thinking** below.

Model Your Thinking

 Comprehension Skill: Theme

Think ALOUD

Every story has a theme. This is the big idea or message about the world or people that the author would like you to learn or think about. This story tells about two friends who quickly lose their temper. Their angry feelings lead to Loon dumping oil on Raven, and Raven hitting Loon with a pot and hurting him. When I read this book, I thought about times when I've gotten angry at a friend. I think the big idea, or theme, is that it is important not to lose your temper because anger can lead to disaster.

After Reading

Revisiting the Text

Comprehension Have small groups discuss the events that led up to the disaster that happened between Raven and Loon. Encourage them to reread the book together and look at the pictures to help them understand the author's theme. They can use the Story Elements organizer on page 144 to record their discussion ideas.

76B
Market Treasure Hunt

by Gail Blasser Riley
Leveled Reader 76B
Genre: Realistic Story
Level: Easy/Average

Summary

Keisha has a chance to enter a contest and invites her best friend Lena to join her in figuring out the clues. Lena is very nervous, but she tries to help. When Keisha wins the contest, she shares the prize with Lena to thank her for her help. She learns that having a good friend is even better than winning a contest.

At a Glance

Links to the Student Edition

✒ **Comprehension Skill:** Theme

Selection Vocabulary: *greedy, feast, brilliant, delighted*

Program Theme: Traditions
Unit Theme: From Past to Present

Good friendships can last a lifetime. A contest shows how two friends can help each other accomplish a goal and gain confidence by working together.

Before Reading

Motivating the Reader
Build Background About Friendship and Cooperation

Ask students to suppose that they have been asked to help find a small item that has been lost in the classroom. Tell them it needs to be found within a certain amount of time. Encourage them to discuss how working with a friend might help them accomplish this task. Then ask students to brainstorm a list of activities and projects that would be easier and more fun to do with a friend.

Preview and Predict

Have students scan the cover, text, and illustrations to get an idea of what the book is about. Encourage students to use the title and illustrations to make predictions about the events which might happen in the book. Suggest students read to find out what happens during the market treasure hunt.

Point out the selection vocabulary and any unfamiliar words, such as *treasure hunters, mercado, nervous, gulped, tapped out,* and *drought,* that might be important to understanding the book. Make sure students are familiar with the rules and purpose of a treasure hunt as described in the book.

During Reading

Guiding Comprehension

Use the following questions to support students as they read.

- **Page 2** What does *treasure hunters* mean? Think about each word in this term. (It means "people who hunt for treasure.")

- **Page 2** What is a *mercado*? (It means "market.")

- **Pages 2–3** How does each character feel about winning a chance to be a treasure hunter? (Keisha is excited. Lena is nervous.)

- **Page 4** What are the rules of the contest? (The girls have eight minutes to find all the clues in the store.)

- **Page 5** Why are the words in the box important? (They show the first clue the girls must solve.) What food do you think the clue is describing? Why? (Encourage students to make logical predictions.) Repeat this question for other clues.

- **Page 6** How do you think Lena is feeling? How do you know? (She is feeling scared or nervous. She gulps, and when she tries to speak, no words come out.)

- **Page 7** What words in the clue gave Keisha the idea to look at the turtle soup? (slow and spoon)

- **Page 11** What word in the clue gives Lena the idea to say the words fast? (speedy) How does this help her solve the clue? (She says the words to the clue quickly, and they form the words *lettuce and tomatoes.*)

- **Page 15** What reasons does Lena give for giving the tickets to Keisha? (Keisha figured out most of the clues, and Fun World is one of her favorite places.)

- **Page 16** Why does Keisha give one ticket back to Lena? (Lena is Keisha's best friend. Lena helped her win the tickets.)

- **Page 16** What is the big idea, or theme, of this story? (Possible answer: Winning is fun, but having a good friend is the best.)

Ongoing Assessment

Reading Strategies

If... a student has difficulty decoding *drought* on page 7,	**Then...** urge the student to use the clue's rhyming pattern.
If... a student gets frustrated trying to solve the clues,	**Then...** tell the student to focus on making logical predictions.
If... a student has trouble identifying the book's theme,	**Then...** use **Model Your Thinking** below.

Model Your Thinking

Think ALOUD

Comprehension Skill: Theme

The theme is a story's big idea. To figure out what the big idea is, I ask myself: "What does the author want me to learn? What lessons do the characters learn?" Sometimes, the author may state the theme in the story. For example, on page 16, Keisha says having a good friend is the best. I think about how these girls treat one another. I think about my own experiences with good friends. The theme of this story is given by Keisha: "Winning is fun. But having a good friend is the best!"

After Reading

Revisiting the Text

Comprehension Write *friendship* in the center of Web 1 on page 132. Have students reread the book and look at the actions and words of Keisha and Lena. Have them record story details around the outer edge of the web, as well as examples of similar experiences they have had with a friend. Have pairs share their webs and work together to write a sentence they feel best tells the book's theme.

77A
The Little Wagon

by Linda Cave
Leveled Reader 77A
Genre: Fantasy
Level: Easy

Summary

An old wagon recalls the fun it had helping Paco, the child who got the wagon as a birthday gift. The wagon reminisces aloud to an appreciative audience of lawn tools and worries about what may happen to him now that Paco has grown up. He is delighted to find he has not been forgotten, and he gets the opportunity to become useful again to Paco and Paco's daughter.

At a Glance

Links to the Student Edition

◎ **Comprehension Skill:** Setting

Selection Vocabulary: *appreciate, scolded, startled*

Program Theme: Traditions
Unit Theme: From Past to Present

An old wagon discovers that he can remain useful and appreciated by a new generation after his first owner grows up.

Before Reading

Motivating the Reader
Build Background About Reusing and Sharing

Ask students to think about favorite objects or toys they have stopped using or needing as they grow older. Invite them to share stories about these possessions and tell what became of these items. Ask them to explain why these items were important in the past and to consider whether some of these items would be useful today or in the future to someone else.

Preview and Predict

Have students scan the cover, text, and illustrations to get an idea of what the book is about. Prepare students to read by drawing their attention to the facial expressions on the pictures of the wagon and other tools on pages 2 and 3. Encourage students to make predictions about what might happen in the book. Suggest they read to find out more about the little wagon.

Point out selection vocabulary and any unfamiliar words, such as *junk pile* and *strangers,* that might be important to understanding the book.

During Reading

Guiding Comprehension

Use the following questions to support students as they read.

- **Pages 2–3** Look at the items pictured here. What are they used for? What kind of room do you think is shown here? (Many of the items are used for lawn and garden care. The room could be a garage or a big tool shed.)

- **Pages 4–5** Describe one thing that the little wagon did to help Paco. (It carried presents to Paco's room. It carried things to the park for his baseball team.)

- **Pages 4–5** Think about how you would feel about someone or something as helpful as the little wagon. What do you think *appreciate* means? (It means "to be thankful for or have a good opinion about someone or something.")

- **Pages 6–7** How did the little wagon help on the camping trip? (It carried camping gear from the car. It carried the tackle box, lunches, and fish.)

- **Page 7** How did the wagon feel about helping Paco and working hard? (It liked working hard for Paco.)

- **Page 10** Why doesn't Paco play with the wagon any more? (Paco grew up and went away.)

- **Page 12** Look at the picture. Why is the wagon startled? (He is being taken apart and worked on, and he is worried he will go to the junk pile.) What other word means the same as *startled*? (surprised, worried)

- **Pages 14–15** Look at the word *stranger* on these pages. Who is the stranger? (Paco) Who do you think the little girl is? (Paco's daughter)

- **Page 16** How does the little wagon feel by the end of the book? Why does he feel this way? (He feels happy because he can now be useful helping Paco's daughter.)

Reading Strategies

If... a student can identify the changes in time from past to present,	**Then...** praise the student for using picture and word clues to understand the setting.
If... a student has difficulty identifying the book's setting,	**Then...** use **Model Your Thinking** below.

Model Your Thinking

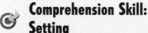 **Comprehension Skill: Setting**

 Think ALOUD

The setting is the time and place in which a story occurs. Sometimes an author will tell you exactly what the setting is, but sometimes you need to use the pictures and details in the story to figure out the setting. For example, in *The Little Wagon*, the author never tells us where the wagon is telling the story. I look back through the pages for clues. On pages 2 and 3, there is a picture of a wagon in a room with lots of tools and a driveway leading out of the door. These are things you might find in a garage, so the setting is probably in a garage. The book tells about two different times. The story the wagon tells is about when Paco was a little boy, but now Paco is a man and his little girl will be using the wagon.

After Reading

Revisiting the Text

Comprehension In this book, the little wagon talks about events that happened in different settings. Have the students reread the book, looking for clues in the pictures and words on each page that tell them where an event takes place. Have students use the Web 2 on page 133 to organize the information they find for each setting. You may want to work on the first one together.

77B
Akiko's Kite

by Cora Plexus
Leveled Reader 77B
Genre: Realistic Story
Level: Easy/Average

Summary

A girl learns some of the history and beliefs about kite flying in Japan as she and her grandmother wait for the wind to blow. The two characters share a day of expectation and discovery as they test Akiko's new kite.

At a Glance

Links to the Student Edition

☞ **Comprehension Skill:** Setting

Selection Vocabulary: *dragon, lucky, rustling*

Program Theme: Traditions
Unit Theme: From Past to Present

Young and old people can learn from and enjoy each other through the practicing and telling of traditions, such as kite flying.

Before Reading

Motivating the Reader
Build Background About Traditions

Explain to students that traditions are things that families or a culture do or believe. These actions and beliefs are passed down from an older generation to younger generations such as from grandparents to grandchildren. Often traditions may happen at the same time every year. Invite students to share ways their family celebrates special holidays. Then ask students to imagine it is a warm spring day. It is warm and breezy and inviting outside. Ask them to think of things they enjoy doing every year on a beautiful spring day.

Preview and Predict

Have students scan the cover, text, and illustrations to get an idea of what the story is about. Prepare students to read by drawing their attention to the book's cover, opening it to show the front and back. Ask them to read the title and to describe what might be happening on the cover. Encourage students to make predictions about the relationship of the two characters shown on the cover and the events which might happen in the book. Students can set their own purposes for reading, such as finding out more about kite flying.

Point out selection vocabulary and any unfamiliar words, such as *celebration, delicate,* and *symbol,* that might be important to understanding the book.

During Reading

Use the following questions to support students as they read.

- **Pages 2–3** *Who are the two characters that are in the story?* (Akiko and her grandmother)

- **Page 2** *What does Akiko see out her window that shows her the weather is nice?* (She sees a blue sky, light wind, and leaves rustling in the trees.)

- **Page 3** *What does Akiko hope will happen today?* (She hopes that she and her grandmother can make Akiko's kite fly, like a bird.)

- **Page 4** *What does delicate mean? Look for clues in the nearby words.* (It means "very thin, easily torn.")

- **Page 7** *What tradition do artists in Japan have in the spring?* (They make beautiful kites for people to fly.)

- **Pages 8–9** *What does the picture in the thought bubble show?* (It shows what Aikiko is trying to imagine—her grandmother as a little girl flying her big fish kite.)

- **Page 11** *What are Akiko and Grandmother waiting for?* (They are waiting for the wind to lift Akiko's kite.)

- **Page 12** *How did people use kites long ago?* (The used kites to send messages.) *What did some people believe about kites?* (They thought kites could connect the sky and the earth.)

- **Pages 14–15** *What action words does the author use to describe the kite's movements?* (swoops, whirls, dances, flies, swirls)

- **Page 16** *What surprise does Grandmother give Aikiko?* (She gives Aikiko the big fish kite she flew when she was a little girl.)

- **Page 16** *Where does this story take place?* (probably in Japan) *What time of year is it?* (spring)

Ongoing Assessment

Reading Strategies

If... a student has difficulty understanding words such as *rustling* on page 16,	**Then...** have them read past the word, looking for explanatory phrases to help them understand the word.
If... a student has difficulty identifying the book's setting,	**Then...** use **Model Your Thinking** below.

Model Your Thinking

 Comprehension Skill: Setting

Think ALOUD

Every story has a setting, which is the time and place in which the story happens. An author does not always tell what the setting is exactly, but there are clues in the pictures, the words, and events which help me figure out where and when the story takes place. The author of *Akiko's Kite* does not say that this story takes place in Japan, but she gives clues that it takes place there. For exampie, on page 5, Grandmother states that every spring artists in Japan fill the sky with colorful kites. Then, on page 10, there is a description and picture of many people waiting to fly kites. The people wear clothing that looks like traditional clothes worn in Japan. These clues tell me that this story probably takes place in Japan during the spring.

After Reading

Revisiting the Text

Comprehension Ask students to reread the book, looking for clues which tell them about the time and place the story is set. Have students use Web 1 on page 132. Have them write the setting in the center and list the clues at the ends of the web lines.

78A

Grandma Giggle

by Milo Mason
Leveled Reader 78A
Genre: Tall Tale
Level: Easy

Summary

This humorous tale of an amazing, unusual, and resourceful grandmother explains how a very long nose can be helpful as well as bothersome. Grandma Giggle's unique nose saves the day as it helps her solve a cooking disaster. While rescuing her baking, she also invents the donut!

Links to the Student Edition

⌖ **Comprehension Skill:** Cause and Effect

Selection Vocabulary: *recipe, measured*

Program Theme: Traditions
Unit Theme: From Past to Present

Tall tales often tell humorous, even outrageous, stories about our past and the origins of things. According to this tale, the present-day donut was invented by a clever grandmother with a really long nose.

Before Reading

Motivating the Reader
Build Background About Exaggeration

Draw a picture of a very tall superhero with long arms and legs. Show a group of clouds around the man's knees. Write the sentence: *Super Tall Ted was so tall that he looked down on a cloud.* Invite volunteers to draw other pictures and write sentences of amazing feats that Super Tall Ted could do. Then ask students to imagine a hero or a heroine with a super long nose. Discuss what life would be like for this character. Ask students to think of the advantages and disadvantages of having a super long nose.

Preview and Predict

Have students scan the cover, text, and illustrations to get an idea of what the story is about. Encourage students to make predictions about who the characters might be and what might happen in the book. Ask them if they think this story tells about something that could really happen or is make-believe, encouraging them to use the illustrations for clues. Suggest students read to find out who Grandma Giggle is and what she does.

Point out selection vocabulary and any unfamiliar words, such as *amazing, handy,* and *ruined,* that might be important to understanding the book.

During Reading

Guiding Comprehension

Use the following questions to support students as they read.

- **Page 2 Do you think this story will tell about something real or is it make believe? How do you know?** (It is make-believe because no one could be as tall as Grandma Giggle, people don't live in teacups, and it is very unlikely to have thirty-two grandchildren all born on the same day.)

- **Page 4 What is the most amazing thing about Grandma?** (She has a really long nose.)

- **Pages 5–7 What problems does Grandma Giggle's nose cause?** (Birds make nests on her nose. She has difficulty looking in a mirror, driving a car, and riding in the elevator because her nose gets in the way.)

- **Page 7 Why was it hard for Grandma Giggle to ride in an elevator?** (Her nose was too long, and it would get stuck in the doors)

- **Page 8 The author says that Grandma's nose "came in handy." What do you think this means?** (Sometimes her nose was useful.) **In what ways is her nose handy?** (She can scratch her own toes [page 4], hang clothes to dry on it, smell things far away, such as roses, rain, and the moon.)

- **Page 9 Why did Grandma Giggle's grandchildren think her nose was perfect? Look at the picture for clues.** (It was long enough to use as a slide.)

- **Page 12 What made the cakes fly out the window?** (Grandma slipped on a banana peel and knocked over the table with the cakes.)

- **Page 13 What does it mean that Grandma Giggle used her head?** (It means she got an idea. It also means she used her head literally by using her nose.)

- **Page 14 How does she save the cakes?** (She catches them on her nose.)

- **Page 16 What kind of food did Grandma Giggle invent?** (donuts)

Reading Strategies

If... a student uses the pictures to help her or him understand what is happening in the text,	**Then...** praise the student for self-monitoring. Ask what clues he or she used to help them figure the story out.
If... a student is unable to tell how Grandma Giggle created donuts,	**Then...** encourage him or her to reread the end of the book, looking carefully at the pictures and text for clues.
If... a student cannot recognize cause-and-effect relationships,	**Then...** use **Model Your Thinking** below.

Model Your Thinking

Think ALOUD

🎯 **Comprehension Skill: Cause and Effect**

Good readers try to figure out what happens in a story and why it happens. They look for causes and effects. A cause tells why something happens, and an effect is what happens. Sometimes a clue word, such as *because* or *so*, signals a cause-and-effect relationship between events. Other times, you have to figure out causes and effects. For example, on page 11, I see Grandma Giggle falling down. I ask myself, "Why did this happen?" I look at the picture and read the words below it. She slipped because she stepped on a banana peel. If I continue to look for reasons why things are happening, I will understand the story better.

After Reading

Revisiting the Text

Comprehension Work with the students to figure out the chain of events that begin on page 10 and eventually lead to the invention of the donut. Use the Cause and Effect organizer on page 145. You may wish to fill in one part of a cause-and-effect relationship to help prompt students.

78B

Crash! Flash!

by Ellen Javernick
Leveled Reader 78B
Genre: Informational Article
Level: Easy/Average

Summary

People's curiosity about thunder and lightning have led to many interesting stories and explanations. After telling a few interesting examples of these tales, this book gives a simple explanation with diagrams showing how thunderstorms are formed and how they affect people and our environment. There are even tips to help readers stay safe during a thunderstorm.

At a Glance

Links to the Student Edition

☞ **Comprehension Skill:** Cause and Effect

Selection Vocabulary: *thunder, lightning, distance, weather*

Program Theme: Traditions
Unit Theme: From Past to Present

Stories explaining the causes and effects of thunderstorms have been passed down from generation to generation.

Before Reading

Motivating the Reader
Build Background About Thunderstorms

Have students use Web 3 on page 134. Have them write *thunderstorms* in the center oval, and then record words or symbols they associate with thunderstorms. Ask them to think about what they see and hear during a storm and how it makes them feel. Students can group similar details in one strand of the web. Invite volunteers to share their webs.

Preview and Predict

Have students scan the cover, text, and illustrations to get an idea of what the story is about. Have them compare the pictures on pages 3, 5, and 6 to the diagrams on pages 8 and 9. Encourage students to make predictions about what kinds of information they might find in the book. Have them think of some questions they have about thunderstorms, and suggest they read to look for the answers to their questions.

Point out selection vocabulary and any unfamiliar words, such as *crystals, electricity,* and *explodes,* that might be important to understanding the book.

During Reading

Guiding Comprehension

Use the following questions to support students as they read.

- **Page 2** How are *crash* and *flash* related to thunder and lightning? (*Crash* is the sound thunder makes. *Flash* refers to the flash of light we see when lightning strikes.)

- **Pages 4–6** What stories have people told to explain what causes thunder to crash? (Some say it is an angry man racing a goat cart across the sky. Some Native Americans say it is made by the flapping wings of a thunderbird. Others say it is the sound of people bowling in the sky or a thunder baby kicking and crying.)

- **Page 8** What happens to warm air as it rises up? (It gets colder.) What does the cold air cause to happen? (The cold air turns tiny drops of water in the cloud into ice crystals.)

- **Page 9** How could you tell by looking at a cloud that it was going to rain? (Clouds get bigger and turn gray right before it begins to rain.)

- **Page 10** What causes lightning? (The electricity from the rain drops jump from one part of a cloud to another part and from a cloud to the ground. These jumping sparks of electricity are lightning.)

- **Page 11** What causes the air to explode? (The lightning makes the air very hot until it explodes as thunder.)

- **Pages 12–13** How many seconds could you count in between the lightning and thunder if the storm was two miles away? (ten seconds)

- **Page 14** How can thunderstorms be helpful? (They cool and clean the air, and they carry water to dry land.) How can they be harmful? (Lightening can hurt people. It can also start fires.)

- **Page 16** Where is the safest place to be during a thunderstorm? (inside)

Reading Strategies

If... a student has difficulty interpreting the diagrams,	**Then...** have the student work with a partner to compare the diagrams to the surrounding text.
If... a student cannot recognize cause-and-effect relationships,	**Then...** use **Model Your Thinking** below.

Model Your Thinking

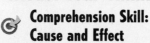 **Comprehension Skill: Cause and Effect**

Think ALOUD

A cause is why something happens, and an effect is what happens. This book describes both real and imaginary causes of thunderstorms. Pages 4–6 tell about stories people told to explain what causes thunder—Pages 8–11 give a scientific reason for the causes of thunder and lightning. As I read, I look at what happens and ask myself. "Why does this happen?" I read that because warm air rises and gets colder, tiny drops of water turn into ice crystals. Asking myself: "What happens?" and "Why does it happen?" helps me better understand the causes and effects of a thunderstorm.

After Reading

Revisiting the Text

Comprehension Have students use the Cause and Effect organizer on page 145. Take a book walk to review the information. Pause at appropriate places to ask: "What happens?" and "Why does it happen?" to help students identify causes and effects in the book.

79A
Flood and Famine

by Sharon Fear
Leveled Reader 79A
Genre: Realistic Story
Level: Easy

Summary

A raja hires an elephant trainer to train his mischievous elephants to behave. His plan works, but he discovers that he and the people miss the excitement of the days before his two elephants were trained. He asks the trainer to untrain the elephants, and palace life is fun once again.

At a Glance

Links to the Student Edition

Comprehension Skill: Compare and Contrast

Selection Vocabulary: *double, palace, reward*

Program Theme: Traditions
Unit Theme: From Past to Present

Sometimes we make changes to make things better. But some things, such as playful elephants, are better left unchanged.

Before Reading

Motivating the Reader
Build Background About Elephants

Show students pictures of elephants in different situations—in the wild, at work with humans, or in a circus. Have students share what they know about elephants, such as what they look like, what noises they make, what they eat, and how they act. Allow children to use words, sounds, or pantomime, or draw pictures to help them share what they know about elephants.

Preview and Predict

Have students scan the cover, text, and illustrations to get an idea of what the book is about. Draw their attention to the elephants' behavior in the illustrations. Encourage students to make predictions about where the story might take place and what will happen. Suggest students set their own purposes for reading, such as finding out the meaning of the title or finding out what happens to the two elephants.

Point out selection vocabulary and any unfamiliar words, such as *flood, famine,* and *frisk,* that might be important to understanding the book.

During Reading

Guiding Comprehension

Use the following questions to support students as they read.

- **Pages 2–3** *How does the story begin?* (A raja offers a reward to anyone who can train two of his elephants. A fine trainer applies for the job.)

- **Page 5** *Why is one of the elephants named Flood?* (It plays in the water and splashes people who come near.)

- **Page 6** *What does the other elephant do that makes the name Famine fit?* (The other elephant is greedy and is always eating. A famine happens when there is no more food left to eat. The raja believe the elephant will eat everything in the palace.)

- **Pages 7–9** *How did the trainer stop the elephants' bad habits?* (He worked them so hard they were too tired to eat or play.)

- **Page 9** *What other word means almost the same as frisk that makes sense in this sentence?* (play, romp)

- **Pages 10–11** *Look at the people in this picture. How are they feeling?* (No one is smiling. One boy is yawning. Another is sleeping. These expressions show they feel sad or bored.)

- **Page 11** *Why aren't things as much fun anymore?* (Without Flood and Famine causing trouble, there is no excitement in the palace.)

- **Page 13** *Find the word remembering. What was it that the raja was remembering?* (He was remembering when his children were happy playing with the elephants.)

- **Page 13** *What do you think the Raja will do?* (Predictions may vary.)

- **Pages 14–16** *What did the raja mean when he asked the trainer to untrain Flood and Famine? How did he want the elephants to act?* (He wanted the trainer to make the elephants act the way they had before he started working with them.)

Reading Strategies

If... a student doesn't understand the raja's request to untrain the elephants,	**Then...** ask the student to think about how adding the prefix *un-* changes the meaning of a base word.
If... a student reads the selection using different inflections for different kinds of sentences,	**Then...** praise him or her for noticing these different types of sentences and reading with expression.
If... a student has difficulty comparing and contrasting characters or events in the book,	**Then...** use **Model Your Thinking** below.

Model Your Thinking

Think ALOUD

🎯 **Comprehension Skill: Compare and Contrast**

When you compare, you tell how two or more things are alike. When you contrast, you tell how they are different. As I read, I try to notice what the author is saying about what life was like in the palace before Flood and Famine were trained, and how it is different after they are trained. Page 5 and 6 describe the elephants' habits before they were trained. Flood likes to splash people. Famine loves to eat. Page 9 shows the elephants after they are trained. They are sleeping and are too tired to splash or eat. By comparing and contrasting how the elephants act before and after training, I can better understand what happens to these characters.

After Reading

Revisiting the Text

Comprehension Have pairs reread the book and use the T-Chart on page 150 to list the elephants' behavior and its effects on palace life when they were trained and untrained.

79B

Raising Chickens

by Barbara Gannett
Leveled Reader 79B
Genre: Realistic Story
Level: Easy/Average

Summary

A young girl learns about the growth and care of chickens by watching her grandmother working in her chicken coop. She is eagerly preparing for the day when Grandma will give her some chicks of her own to raise. Both the grandmother and granddaughter share a love for these animals.

At a Glance

Links to the Student Edition

Comprehension Skill: Compare and Contrast

Selection Vocabulary: *grain, single, thief*

Program Theme: Traditions
Unit Theme: From Past to Present

A grandmother passes down her knowledge and love of chickens to her granddaughter.

Before Reading

Motivating the Reader
Build Background About Chickens

Draw a word web on the chalkboard and write *Chickens* in the center. Invite volunteers to write words or draw pictures of things related to chickens in the web's outer circles. Show students pictures of different kinds of chickens and explain the difference between a hen, a rooster, and a chick. Discuss what it takes to raise and care for chickens as they read the book. Have students work in pairs to write one fact they know about chickens.

Preview and Predict

Have students scan the cover, text, and illustrations to get an idea of what the book is about. Prepare students to read by drawing their attention to the book's cover, opening it to show the front and back. Ask them to read the title and to describe what the girl is doing on the cover. Encourage students to make predictions about what might happen in the book and what things they might learn about raising chickens. Suggest students read to find out if their predictions are correct.

Point out selection vocabulary and any unfamiliar words, such as those related to chickens, that might be important to understanding the book.

During Reading

Guiding Comprehension

Use the following questions to support students as they read.

- **Page 2** Who is telling the story? (The little girl in the picture who is the granddaughter of the older woman.)

- **Pages 2–3** How does the girl know Grandma loves chickens? (Her grandmother names each of her chickens.)

- **Page 5** How do chickens drink? (They dip their beaks in water, and then tip their heads up and swallow.)

- **Page 6** How does a flyway keep the chickens safe? (A flyway is surrounded by chicken wire. Animals can't get in the flyway to harm the chickens.)

- **Page 7** Why does Grandma call the biggest hen a "big thief"? (It always chases the little ones away and eats most of the food.)

- **Page 9** How is Grandma's farm like a chicken ranch? (They both raise chickens.) How is her farm different from a chicken ranch? (Grandma's farm is much smaller. It has fewer chickens, and her chickens have more space.)

- **Page 10** How do the chicks stay warm? (The heat from a light bulb keeps them warm.)

- **Pages 13–14** What happens to the eggs on the farm? (Grandma sells some, eats some, and lets some of them hatch.)

- **Page 15** Why are the girl and her father building a chicken house? (The girl, will use it to raise the chicks that her grandma is giving her.)

- **Page 16** How are the girl and Grandma alike? (Both of them love chickens.)

Reading Strategies

If... a student is confused by the two meanings of *down,*	**Then...** have the student compare its use on pages 10 and 11 and restate each sentence in his or her own words.
If... a student has difficulty comparing and contrasting,	**Then...** use **Model Your Thinking** below.

Model Your Thinking

 Comprehension Skill: Compare and Contrast

Think ALOUD

Comparing means telling how two things are alike. Contrasting means telling how two things are different. Good readers can better understand new information by comparing and contrasting it to what they already know. For example, to understand how a chicken drinks, I can compare and contrast the description on page 5 to what I already know about how a dog or a cat drinks. Authors also compare and contrast things in a story to help readers understand them. For instance, on page 9, I read that Grandma has about 50 chickens on her farm and that thousands live at chicken ranches. That is one way ranches and farms are different.

After Reading

Revisiting the Text

Comprehension Have pairs reread the book and use the Venn Diagram on page 147 to compare and contrast chicken ranches and Grandma's farm, Grandma and the narrator, or chicks and chickens. Have students list differences in the outer section of each circle and similarities in the overlapping center.

80A
The Fisherman and the Fish

retold by Anne Phillips
Leveled Reader 80A
Genre: Fable
Level: Easy

Summary

A fisherman learns a valuable lesson from a very special fish. As the fish grants the fisherman's wishes, the fisherman becomes more dissatisfied and greedy. After living in a house, a grand house, and a castle, he finds himself once again in his leaky old hut, but with a new appreciation for what he has.

At a Glance

Links to the Student Edition

⟳ **Comprehension Skill:** Predicting

Selection Vocabulary: *astonished, cruel, shone, thirst*

Program Theme: Traditions
Unit Theme: From Past to Present

A fisherman shows that it's never too late to learn from past mistakes.

Before Reading

Motivating the Reader
Build Background About Positive Attitudes

Ask students to imagine they have just been stranded on a desert island. They have pieces of wood from the shipwreck, a few pieces of clothing, and a basket of food and water. Ask them to role-play two different scenarios. In the first, ask two volunteers to act in a negative, unappreciative way, complaining about their circumstances. Ask the students to discuss whether this would help their situation. Encourage students to discuss ways the characters could talk and act which would help them survive. Then have a few volunteers act out the same scene using students' suggestions.

Preview and Predict

Have students scan the cover, text, and illustrations. Tell them that a *fable* is a short story which teaches a lesson and usually includes animals that talk. Encourage students to make predictions about what might happen in the book. Students can record their predictions using the T-Chart on page 150, recording predictions on the left and reasons for their predictions on the right. Encourage students to read to find out if their predictions are correct, revising them as needed.

Point out selection vocabulary and any unfamiliar words, such as *cast, grand,* and *greedy,* that might be important to understanding the book.

During Reading

Guiding Comprehension

Use the following questions to support students as they read.

- **Page 2** What kind of home does the fisherman live in? (It is a tiny hut with a leaky roof.)

- **Page 3** What do you think *cast* means? What other word makes sense in this sentence? (to throw something; threw, tossed)

- **Page 3** What made the fisherman think it would be cruel to eat the fish? (It was an unusual and pretty fish.)

- **Page 4** Why does the fish feel lucky? (The fisherman decided not to eat the fish, and he put the fish back in the sea.) What does the fish do to thank the fisherman? (He makes the fisherman's wish for a better house come true.)

- **Page 5** What word did the fisherman use to describe his new house? (wonderful)

- **Pages 6–7** What does the fisherman do next? (He grows tired of his house and eating bread, so he demands a bigger house and new food from the fish.)

- **Page 9** What do you think will happen next? Why? (The fisherman will demand a bigger house and different food from the fish. This is what he did the last time he got bored.)

- **Page 11** How does the fisherman's feelings for his new house change? Which words show this change? (At first he is excited, but then he gets bored. The words *then he got tired* show this change.)

- **Pages 13–14** The fisherman says he was greedy. What does *greedy* mean? The fish gives a clue about this word on page 13. (It means "to want too much.")

- **Page 16** What lesson does the fisherman learn? (Possible answers: He learns to be thankful for what he has because it is better than nothing. If you get too greedy, you can lose everything.)

Reading Strategies

If... a student has difficulty understanding the word *grand* on page 8,	**Then...** have her or him compare the "grand" house with the houses on pages 2 and 5.
If... a student makes good predictions as he or she reads,	**Then...** praise the student for noticing and understanding story clues.
If... a student has difficulty making accurate predictions,	**Then...** use **Model Your Thinking** below.

Model Your Thinking

Comprehension Skill: Predicting

Think ALOUD

When I predict, I tell what might happen next in a story. Predicting helps me make sense of the story, and makes me eager to read on. Good readers use what has already happened in the story and what they know from real life to help them make good predictions. For instance, after reading up through page 10, I noticed that the fisherman repeats almost the same words to the fish. Each time, he asks for a bigger home and something different to eat. I remembered that the fish granted his wish before, so I predicted that the fisherman would go home and find an even bigger home and different food. As I read on to page 11, I checked to see if my predictions were right. I keep making and checking my predictions as I read the rest of the book.

After Reading

Revisiting the Text

Comprehension Have the students share the predictions they recorded in their T-Charts before and while reading the book. Discuss with students their reasons for making the predictions they did and whether their predictions were correct.

80B

The Time Machine

by Fay Robinson
Leveled Reader 80B
Genre: Science Fiction
Level: Easy/Average

Summary

Jenny takes a trip in a time machine, hoping the future will bring fewer rules and maybe even better dinners! She finds the future interesting and fun, but she soon discovers that parents still want respect, children still have music practice and homework, and the meals aren't much tastier. The trip leads to a new appreciation of the present.

At a Glance

Links to the Student Edition

Comprehension Skill: Predicting

Selection Vocabulary: *arrived, excitement, respect, spied*

Program Theme: Traditions
Unit Theme: From Past to Present

At first, living in a different time and place may seem very appealing. After a closer look, you may find an appreciation of where you are now.

Before Reading

Motivating the Reader
Build Background About the Future and the Past

Ask students to describe what life is like now for someone their age. Have students think about what clothes they wear, what they do for fun, what they do in school, and what chores they do at home. Write *Present* on the chalkboard, and list their ideas underneath. Then organize students into two groups. Have one group make a similar list for the past, and have the other group make a list for the future. Groups can share their lists and discuss in which time period they would like to live.

Preview and Predict

Have students scan the cover, text, and illustrations. Prepare students to read by drawing their attention to the machine on the book's cover. Discuss what students know about time machines and science fiction stories.

Point out selection vocabulary and any unfamiliar words that might be important to understanding the book. Write these words in the box at the top of the Story Prediction organizer on page 131. Encourage students to use these words and their previewing scan to predict who and what the book might be about. Suggest they read to find out if their predictions are correct.

During Reading

Guiding Comprehension

Use the following questions to support students as they read.

- **Page 3** What would the narrator of the story like to eat for dinner every night? (burgers and fries)

- **Page 4** What do think the sentence "respect your parents" means? Think about how the parents would like the narrator to act. (It means you should listen to your parents, do what your parents tell you to do, and don't talk back to them.)

- **Pages 4–5** Look at the narrator's face and the words she says. How does the narrator feel? (She is unhappy. She doesn't want to do what her mom tells her to do and she's mad at her sister.)

- **Page 6** What do you think Mom said? ("Respect your parents.")

- **Page 6** Do you think the narrator should act and talk the way she does? Why or why not? (No. She is being rude to her parents. The things the parents want her to do are things that are good for her, so she shouldn't complain so much.)

- **Pages 10–11** How does Jenny feel about the future so far? (She feels excited and thinks the future is great.)

- **Pages 12–11** Is life in the future very different from Jenny's life back home? Why or why not? (No. Jenny doesn't like the meal, and Neo's parents expect him to practice his music and be more respectful. These things are like things Jenny experienced at home.)

- **Page 13** What do you think will happen next? (Possible answers: Jenny will find more similarities to life back home. She will decide to go home.)

- **Page 16** Why does Jenny say "there's no time like now"? (She likes the present better than the future.)

Reading Strategies

If... a student has difficulty identifying who is telling the story,	**Then...** ask the student to reread page 2 and page 15 to find clues to tell who is speaking.
If... a student has difficulty decoding multisyllabic words, such as the word *ordinary* on page 9,	**Then...** encourage her or him to divide the word into syllables and pronounce the word syllable by syllable.
If... a student has difficulty making accurate predictions,	**Then...** use **Model Your Thinking** below.

Model Your Thinking

Think ALOUD

🎯 **Comprehension Skill: Predicting**

Predicting means to tell what you think might happen next in a story. Good readers pause and make predictions as they read to help them think about what is happening in the story. Then they keep reading to see if the predictions they made are correct. As I read a story, I think about what I have already read and what I already know about the subject of the story. For instance, I know that the title of this story is *The Time Machine*. This tells me that probably at least one character is going to take a trip through time. Because Jenny seems so frustrated, I predict that she would like to go on a trip to a different time. I read on to see if my prediction is correct.

After Reading

Revisiting the Text

Comprehension Ask students to refer to the Story Prediction organizers they completed before reading the book. Invite them to discuss what clues they used to make their predictions and how accurate their predictions were.

81A
Mikey's Garden

by Bonita Rio Ferraro
Leveled Reader 81A
Genre: Animal Fantasy
Level: Easy

Summary

Mikey falls asleep while working in the garden. When he wakes, he finds himself in a strange and fantastic world where he changes sizes. Mikey feels lost and stranded in places that seem to him like giant sand dunes, thick forests, and deep, dark holes. All alone, Mikey must decide whether to trust the different animals that offer him help. The animals help Mikey find his way home, and Mikey gives each hero a special thank-you gift.

At a Glance

Links to the Student Edition

☞ **Comprehension Skill:** Making Judgments

Selection Vocabulary: *route, soars*

Program Theme: Journeys in Time and Space
Unit Theme: Are We There Yet?

Being alone can be scary, but sometimes traveling away from the usual places gives you a chance to practice making choices.

Before Reading

Motivating the Reader
Build Background About Friends Who Help

Invite students to share their experiences of times when they had a problem and a friend helped them solve it. Ask them how they felt before they got help and how they felt after they got help. Discuss ways we can thank those who help us. Record students' ideas on the chalkboard.

Preview and Predict

Have students scan the cover, text, and illustrations to get an idea of what the book is about. Return to the cover and ask students to identify the garden and tell who they think the book's main character will be. Encourage students to look at the illustrations and make predictions about the kinds of problems this character may face. Suggest they read to find out what Mikey's garden is like.

Point out selection vocabulary and any unfamiliar words, such as *wondered* and *scampered,* that might be important to understanding the book.

During Reading

Guiding Comprehension

Use the following questions to support students as they read.

- **Page 2** Look at the words *Crunch, Chomp, and Clomp. What do these words mean? What do they tell you about Mikey's garden work?* (They describe the sounds of Mikey's work. They tell you his work is noisy and hard.)

- **Pages 4–5** What do you think has happened to Mikey? (Mikey has shrunk to the size of an ant. He thinks he is all alone on a giant sand hill until an ant shows him a route over the ant hill.)

- **Page 5** What decision does Mikey have to make? (He has to decide whether or not to follow the ant.) Is this what you would decide to do if you were Mikey? Why or why not? (Yes. He needs help, and the ant seems nice. No. The ant is a stranger, and Mikey should find his own way over the hill.) Ask similar questions about other decisions Mikey makes.

- **Page 7** What does Mikey think about before deciding to go with the bird? (He thinks he will feel scared and alone if the bird soars away without him.)

- **Page 8** Look at the words *My hero. Who is Mikey talking about? Why does he say this?* (He's talking about the bird who helped him. He is saying thank you to the bird.)

- **Pages 12–14** What does Mikey give the squirrel as thanks for helping him? (He gives him a nut.) Can you find the other gifts Mikey gives in the book? How does he choose each gift? (He also gives bread, seeds, a bone, and some vegetables away. He chooses a gift that each character would like to eat.)

- **Page 15** What happens to end Mikey's adventures? How does the picture tell you that the adventures are over? (Mikey's mom calls him. He looks the right size now and he's standing back near his house.)

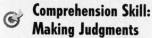

Reading Strategies

If... a student is confused by the sudden jumps in setting on pages 4, 7, 9, and 13,	Then... remind him or her that strange things can happen in make-believe stories.
If... a student stumbles over the word *scampered* on page 10,	Then... share descriptions of how squirrels move and point out the squirrel in the picture.
If... a student has difficulty making reasonable judgments,	Then... use **Model Your Thinking** below.

Model Your Thinking

Comprehension Skill: Making Judgments

Think ALOUD

Characters in stories often have to make choices—just like you and I do. This is called making judgments. Good readers also make judgments about stories. I think about whether a character is kind or mean, brave or foolish. I think about whether I agree with the choices he or she makes. For example, when Mikey asks himself whether to follow an ant, he's making a judgment about whether he can trust the ant. As I read, I make a judgment about whether I agree with Mikey. I ask myself: "Would I do what Mikey does in this situation?" Because the ant seems friendly and is offering to help, I decide that Mikey's choice to follow the ant is right.

After Reading

Revisiting the Text

Comprehension Ask volunteers to take turns role-playing Mikey and the other animals as other students follow the story in their books. Pause at each point where Mikey must make a decision. Discuss Mikey's judgments. If students disagree with Mikey, challenge them to role-play another solution.

81B
A Foggy Flight

by Rory Thomas
Leveled Reader 81B
Genre: Biography
Level: Easy/Average

Summary

Flying twenty-four miles in an airplane should be easy. Unless you're Louis Blériot flying in an airplane without many instruments, compasses, or radar. This nonfiction book takes readers along on the first flight across the English Channel from France to England. It also gives them a very vivid picture of Louis Blériot's personal experience alone in the fog.

At a Glance

Links to the Student Edition

⌖ **Comprehension Skill:** Making Judgments

Selection Vocabulary: *engine, instruments, compasses, flight*

**Program Theme: Journeys in Time and Space
Unit Theme: Are We There Yet?**

Traveling even a short distance, like across the English Channel, can be dangerous and scary.

Before Reading

Motivating the Reader

Build Background About Flight

Display pictures of modern and historical airplanes, making sure to include the open cock-pit propeller planes of Louis Blériot's era. Ask students to name people they associate with airplane flight. Then ask volunteers to describe the various airplanes. Discuss how airplanes have changed over time and brainstorm the challenges of flying in the earliest airplanes. Write *Problems of Early Flight* in the center of Web 1 on page 132. Have students list ideas at the ends of the outer spokes and then share their webs.

Preview and Predict

Have students scan the cover, text, and illustrations to get an idea of what the book is about. Ask them to make predictions about who and what the story is about. Prepare students to read by saying:

> The first sentence in this book tells me a person's name. The page also has a large date at the bottom. These clues hint that this book is about a real person who lived in 1909. Read to find out more about this man and what he did in 1909.

Point out selection vocabulary and any unfamiliar words, such as *propeller* and *fog,* that might be important to understanding the book.

During Reading

Guiding Comprehension

Use the following questions to support students as they read.

- **Page 2** What is Louis Blériot's goal? (to fly across the English Channel) Why does he want to make this flight? (No one else has done it.)

- **Page 2** When does this flight take place? How do you know? (It takes place on July 25, 1909. This date is shown in the picture.)

- **Page 3** Look at this picture. What do you think the dotted line shows? (It shows Louis Blériot's flight path.)

- **Page 4** How does Louis feel about the flight? How do you know? (He is worried. He asks himself "Can I make it?" Since no one has done it before, it is probably something dangerous.)

- **Page 7** Look at the words *Once, twice, three times.* What do they mean? What is Alfred doing? (Alfred has to spin the propeller three times by hand before it makes the engine start.)

- **Pages 10–11** How has the weather changed since Louis began his trip? What problems might the weather cause for Louis? (It has become foggy. Now Louis doesn't know which way to fly to reach England.)

- **Pages 12–13** How does the rainy weather help Louis? (It cools the hot engine.)

- **Pages 14–15** How does Louis's trip end? (He arrives safely in England.)

- **Page 16** How does Louis feel at the end of his trip? (He feels tired and cold, but happy.) What is special about Louis's trip? (He is the first person to fly across the English Channel.)

Reading Strategies

If... a student doesn't recognize the nonfiction format while reading,	Then... highlight the date, map, and factual information on pages 2 and 3.
If... a student has difficulty making reasonable judgments about the book's ideas,	Then... use **Model Your Thinking** below.

Model Your Thinking

 Comprehension Skill: Making Judgments

When you form an opinion about people, events, or ideas in a book, you are making judgments. Good readers look at the words and pictures in books to help them make judgments. They also think about their own experiences—asking themselves what they would do in a similar situation. For example, I look at the dangers Louis Blériot faces to fly the English Channel. I also think about how scared I would be in an open airplane flying through fog. This helps me make the judgment that Louis Blériot is a brave man who likes adventure. I'm not sure I would risk my life just to be the first person to fly across the English Channel.

After Reading

Revisiting the Text

Comprehension Use the T-Chart on page 150. Write *What Louis Blériot Does/How He Feels* on the left side. Write *What I Would Do/How I Would Feel* on the right side. Have students list details about Louis's decisions, actions, and feelings on the left and then imagine what they would do or how they would feel if they were Louis. Ask students to debate whether they think it is a good idea for someone to risk danger to do what no one else has done before. Encourage students to use their charts and other examples to support their judgments.

82A
Gone!

by Patricia Walsh
Leveled Reader 82A
Genre: Narrative Nonfiction
Level: Easy

Summary

A nature photographer leads her companion (and readers) on a walking tour of three marsh areas. She directs her companion to observe and then photograph birds and animals living in wetlands, grassy fields, and woodlands. This book shows what each of these marsh creatures looks like and also tells interesting facts about their living and feeding habits.

At a Glance

Links to the Student Edition

🎯 **Comprehension Skill:** Fact and Opinion

Selection Vocabulary: *spring, ducklings, nest, splash*

Program Theme: Journeys in Time and Space
Unit Theme: Are We There Yet?

Journeys through natural environments, such as marshes, can tell us a lot about the creatures that live in these places.

Before Reading

Motivating the Reader
Build Background About Nature Walks

If possible, post photographs of different marsh environments, or any other available natural surrounding, around the classroom. Invite students to walk through the "nature." Ask them how they think nature walkers should behave and what kinds of skills and tasks walkers might need. Ask students how taking pictures of the natural surroundings might be useful. Discuss students' ideas and post some "nature walk" reminders on the chalkboard.

Preview and Predict

Have students scan the full cover, text, and illustrations to get an idea of what the book is about. Ask them to read the title and predict what is "gone." Point out the use of *I* at the beginning of page 2 and the illustration to establish who the narrator is. Discuss the map on page 3 and the other illustrations to clarify the setting. Then help students predict how the story will unfold and what the main character is doing. Suggest students set their own purpose for reading, such as reading to find out more about the places and animals shown in the book

Point out selection vocabulary and any unfamiliar words, such as *camera* and *marsh,* that might be important to understanding the book. Urge students to reread and study context clues to understand unknown words about nature.

During Reading

Guiding Comprehension

Use the following questions to support students as they read.

- **Pages 2–3** *Who is telling this story?* (The woman shown on page 2 is telling the story.) *What do you think the book will be about?* (It will be about what the narrator and her friend will see on their hike.)

- **Page 3** *What does the curving line on the map show?* (It shows the path of the hike.)

- **Pages 4–5** *What do the woman and the child see?* (They see a great blue heron.) *What is one fact you find out about the great blue heron?* (Answers should reflect the text.) *What opinion does the narrator give about the great blue heron?* (She says it is one of the most beautiful birds in the marsh.) Ask similar questions about the other animals the characters see.

- **Page 5** *What do these last three words on the page mean?* (*Squawk* is the sound of the bird. *Click* is the sound of the camera. *Gone* means the bird has flown away.)

- **Page 6** *Why do you think it's important to be quiet while watching from the bridge?* (Noise might disturb the animals in the pond.)

- **Pages 10–11** *Where are the hikers now? What birds do they see?* (They are in the grassy fields. They see red-winged blackbirds.) *How are male and female blackbirds different?* (The males are black with red patches; the females are dusty brown.)

- **Page 15** *What animals did the hikers learn about? What will help the hikers remember their trip?* (They learned about great blue herons, muskrats, ducklings, red-winged blackbirds, and white-tailed deer. The photographs they took will help them remember what they saw.)

- **Page 16** *Which animal did you find most interesting? Why?* (Encourage well-supported answers.)

Reading Strategies

If... a student cannot visualize the story setting and sequence,	**Then...** encourage him or her to refer frequently to the map on page 3 for help.
If... a student has difficulty distinguishing statements of fact and opinion,	**Then...** use **Model Your Thinking** below.

Model Your Thinking

 Comprehension Skill: Fact and Opinion

Think ALOUD

This book gives me a lot of information about marshes. It also tells me what the photographer thinks about the marshes. As I read, I think about which statements are facts and which are opinions. Statements of fact tell something that can be proved true or false. I could prove that great blue herons live in marshes by reading, watching, or asking an expert about the birds. Statements of opinion tell what someone believes or feels. They cannot be proved true or false. For example, on page 5, the text says the great blue heron is "one of the most beautiful birds in the marsh." This sentence tells what the photographer believes, so I know this is a statement of opinion.

After Reading

Revisiting the Text

Comprehension Assign groups to reread the information about a specific animal. Have them find both statements of fact and opinion about this animal. Groups can record their findings in the T-Chart on page 150. Ask groups to present their findings and tell how they determined which statements were facts and which were opinions.

82B

The Big Hand-off

by Babs Bell Hajdusiewicz
Leveled Reader 82B
Genre: Informational Article
Level: Easy/Average

Summary

Have you ever wondered what happens to a letter when you drop it in the mailbox? This informative book answers this and other questions about mail service. It follows a letter from mailing through the many people and machines that help it reach its final destination. Along the way, readers learn about the ways mail is sorted and routed for the quickest delivery.

At a Glance

Links to the Student Edition

 Comprehension Skill: Fact and Opinion

Selection Vocabulary: *avenue, pool*

Program Theme: Journeys in Time and Space
Unit Theme: Are We There Yet?

People and machines help information, such as letters, travel great distances in today's world.

Before Reading

Motivating the Reader
Build Background About Letters

Show students several pieces of mail, including postcards, letters, catalogs, and if possible, a small package. Invite students to name as many parts of the mail as they can, such as the stamp, label, postmark, and so on. Have a student draw an outline of an envelope on the chalkboard, and ask volunteers to complete its parts with an imaginary address, return address, stamps, and so on. Have students use the Steps in a Process organizer on page 148 to list ideas about how mail travels from sender to recipient. Encourage students to keep their organizers for reference during and after reading the book.

Preview and Predict

Have students scan the cover, text, and illustrations to get an idea of what the book is about. Prepare students to read by drawing their attention to the book's cover, opening it to show the front and back. Ask them to read the title and predict what "the big hand-off" might be. Discuss what students think they may learn from reading this book. Suggest they read to find out how a letter gets from the writer to its final destination.

Point out selection vocabulary and any unfamiliar words, such as *envelope, bins,* and *ZIP code,* that might be important to understanding the book.

During Reading

Guiding Comprehension

Use the following questions to support students as they read.

- **Pages 2–3** *What is the boy doing in these pictures?* (He is addressing an envelope.) *What is the Big Hand-off?* (It is the way a letter gets from the letter writer's hands to the hands of the person addressed on the envelope.)

- **Pages 4–5** *Look at the pictures. Why are they inside cloud shapes? What does the dashed line connecting them mean?* (They are images of the mailing process. The line connects the images to show the sequence of the mailing process.)

- **Page 6** *Who is the first person to touch the letter?* (the mail carrier)

- **Page 8** *What marks are put on the letter by machine? What do these marks mean?* (A machine puts wavy lines on the stamp to show it has been used. It puts a round postmark to show when and where the letter originated.)

- **Pages 9–10** *What do the first two numbers in a ZIP code show?* (The first number shows the area of the country, and the second number shows the nearest city.)

- **Page 11** *Why do letters go on an airplane?* (If letters are going to faraway places, then an airplane can deliver them faster.)

- **Pages 12–14** *How does the letter get from a large post office to the one nearest the letter writer's friend?* (Letters are sorted again at the large post office and put into bins. The bins are put on trucks and are taken to smaller post offices.)

- **Page 16** *What happens to the letter at the end of the book?* (It is delivered to the letter writer's friend.)

Reading Strategies

If... a student stumbles over book's direct address format,	**Then...** encourage him or her to think of the book as a story told to him or her by a friend.
If... a student cannot follow the mail delivery process,	**Then...** help him or her list each step in the letter's journey or refer back to the illustration on pages 4–5.
If... a student has difficulty distinguishing statements of fact and opinion,	**Then...** use **Model Your Thinking** below.

Model Your Thinking

🎯 **Comprehension Skill: Fact and Opinion**

This book tells about how the mail is delivered. It contains mostly statements of fact. Statements of fact can be proved true or false. For example, on pages 9 and 10, the author explains how ZIP codes are used. You could prove whether these statements are true by looking in a book, going to a post office yourself, or asking someone who knows a lot about the postal service. Statements of opinion tell what someone believes or feels. If I say, "This book provides very useful information about the postal service." that is a statement of my opinion.

After Reading

Revisiting the Text

Comprehension Have groups reread the book and list the steps of the Big Hand-off in the Steps in a Process organizer on page 148. Have students use their organizers to discuss interesting statements of fact. Then encourage students to state their own opinions about the process, using the sentence starter: "I think . . . ."

83A
Elli on Her Own
A Fairy Tale

by Linda Yoshizawa
Leveled Reader 83A
Genre: Fairy Tale
Level: Easy

Summary

In this modern-day Cinderella story, a young woman works in the home of two wealthy girls. When the girls are invited to the mayor's ball, Elli is determined to go also. She has to overcome many problems, but Elli finally makes it to the ball where the mayor's handsome son falls in love with her. However, Elli decides a new business, not the son, is what she needs to live happily ever after.

At a Glance

Links to the Student Edition

↻ **Comprehension Skill:** Predicting

Selection Vocabulary: *whirled, snatched, whipped, stumble*

Program Theme: Journeys in Time and Space
Unit Theme: Are We There Yet?

Creative problem solving can be your ticket to a better situation in life.

Before Reading

Motivating the Reader
Build Background About Cinderella

To help students better appreciate this modern-day Cinderella tale, read aloud the classic tale. Have students complete the left half of the Story Comparison organizer on page 140. Discuss Cinderella's problem and how she solves it. Encourage students, as they read, to compare events and characters in the classic tale to the events and characters of *Elli on Her Own*. Students can complete the right side of the organizer after reading the book.

Preview and Predict

Have students scan the cover, text, and illustrations. Point out the diary format of the book. Write the title and list selection vocabulary and other key words or phrases from the book in the Story Prediction organizer on page 131. Encourage students to make predictions about the book based on these words and phrases. Students can return to these organizers when they finish reading the book. Suggest students read to find out what problem Elli has and how she solves it.

During Reading

Guiding Comprehension

Use the following questions to support students as they read.

- **Pages 2–3** Look at this picture. How does it relate to the words? (It shows the experiences Elli writes about in her diary.)

- **Page 2** What does the phrase "beauty is as beauty does" mean? Think about how the girls in the family act. (It means that you aren't really beautiful if you don't act well. The girls don't look good when they are being rude or messy.)

- **Page 3** What problems does Elli have? (She works too hard. She has no free time. The family makes fun of her because she gets so tired and dirty from working.)

- **Pages 4–5** How does Elli feel about being left out of the mayor's ball? (She feels sad.)

- **Page 8** How does Elli solve her problem about needing a new dress? (She finds a mail-order catalog and buys her dress online using the computer.)

- **Pages 10–11** What happens at the ball? (Elli meets and charms the mayor's son. When she has to hurry home, she leaves a slipper behind.) What do you think will happen next? (Students familiar with *Cinderella* may predict that the mayor's son will use the slipper to find Elli.)

- **Page 13** What happens when Elli tries on the glass slipper? (It falls off her foot and breaks.)

- **Pages 14–16** What does the light bulb over Elli's head mean? (It means she has a great idea.) What is Elli's great idea? (She opens a store selling plastic slippers that won't break.)

- **Pages 14–16** Use what you know about *Cinderella* and other fairy tales. How is the ending of this book like or unlike these fairy tales? (Like: It ends happily. Unlike: Elli solves her problems on her own. She doesn't need a fairy godmother or a prince to live happily ever after.)

Model Your Thinking

 Comprehension Skill: Predicting

 Think ALOUD

Telling what you think will happen next in a book is called predicting. Good readers use clues from what they have already read and what they know from their own lives to predict what will happen next. For example, on page 7, I predict that Elli will find a dress for the ball. My clues are that she seems like a very good problem solver. Also, I know that in the original Cinderella story, the girl does go to the ball. As I continue to read, I check whether my predictions are correct and revise or make new predictions about what will happen to Elli. Predicting helps me follow story events and makes me eager to read on.

After Reading

Revisiting the Text

Comprehension Have students look at the Story Prediction organizers they completed before reading the book. Ask students to share some of the predictions they made and explain why they made the predictions they did. Poll students to see how many were surprised by the book's ending. Students can also complete the Story Comparison organizers they began before reading to understand better the similarities and differences between the two texts.

83B
Snowflake
A Sled Dog

by Sharon Gordon
Leveled Reader 83B
Genre: Informational Article
Level: Easy/Average

Summary

Snowflake is a sled dog in the frozen Arctic. When she has puppies, they must learn to be sled dogs too. By following the puppies' training, readers learn about the skills sled dogs need and the ways people teach them to use those skills. The book tells about the important jobs sled dogs perform and some of the problems they must face.

At a Glance

Links to the Student Edition

⌖ **Comprehension Skill:** Predicting

Selection Vocabulary: *howling, wind*

Program Theme: Journeys in Time and Space
Unit Theme: Are We There Yet?

The journeys sled dogs make are sometimes very important. They must learn special skills to travel quickly and safely.

Before Reading

Motivating the Reader
Build Background About Sled Dog Travel

Ask students to imagine that they live in a place where it is so cold that the ground is usually covered with snow or ice. Ask students how they might travel to school or to a friend's house over frozen ground. If needed, point out the option of using dogs pulling sleds, and explain that in some northern places travel by dog-drawn sled has been very useful. Invite students to draw a dog-drawn sled and explain how it works.

Preview and Predict

Have students scan the cover, text, and illustrations to get an idea of what the book is about. Ask them to read the title and predict which dog in the illustration is Snowflake. Encourage students to make predictions about what might happen to Snowflake and the other dogs in the book. Have students write or draw pictures to show their predictions. Encourage students to read to find out if their predictions are correct.

Point out selection vocabulary and any unfamiliar words, such as *mushers, trainers,* and *leader,* that might be important to understanding the book.

During Reading

Guiding Comprehension

Use the following questions to support students as they read.

- **Pages 2–3** Which dog is Snowflake? How do you know? (The large dog is Snowflake. The pictures show you and words tell you that the other dogs are Snowflake's puppies.)

- **Page 3** What do sled dog puppies like to do? (They like to play. They like run and pull.)

- **Pages 4–5** How do sled dogs help people living in the Arctic? (They pull sleds over ice or snow when other kinds of vehicles cannot.)

- **Pages 6–7** What words does the author use to describe full-grown sled dogs? (strong, smart)

- **Page 8** What are mushers? (They are the people who race using sled dogs.)

- **Page 9** What is Snowflake's main job? (She pulls sleds full of food or medicine.)

- **Page 11** What do you predict will happen to the puppies as they grow older? (They will learn how to pull a sled.)

- **Page 11** What is the most important thing the puppies must learn? How does this picture show them learning it? (They must learn to work as a team. The picture shows them learning how to walk when linked together.)

- **Page 14** Look at the words *haw, gee,* and *whoa.* What do they mean? Why do trainers use them? (They mean "left," "right," and "stop." Trainers use them to tell sled dogs what to do.)

- **Page 16** What has happened to the puppies by the end of the book? What do you think will happen to them now? (They have gotten bigger and have learned more about being sled dogs. They will soon be able to take real trips.)

Reading Strategies

If... a student stumbles over the word *mushers* on page 8,	**Then...** direct him or her to the explanation in the text.
If... a student has difficulty making accurate predictions,	**Then...** use **Model Your Thinking** below.

Model Your Thinking

Think
ALOUD

Comprehension Skill: Predicting

Predicting means telling what you think will happen next in a story. Good readers think about what they have read and what they know from their own lives to help them make good predictions. I begin making predictions before I even begin reading by quickly looking at the cover, text, and the pictures in the book to tell what it will be about. I keep making predictions as I read to tell what will happen next. As I continue reading, I check to see if my predictions are correct. Sometimes I change my predictions if new information that I've read changes my mind about what will happen next. For example, at first I thought Snowflake might pull a sled in a race because I know sled dogs are used in races. But then I learned she works carrying food and medicine.

After Reading

Revisiting the Text

Comprehension Have students share the predictions they made before they read the book. Discuss what clues and prior knowledge helped them make these predictions. Then have groups use what they now know about sled dogs to extend the story to tell what might happen to Snowflake's pups.

84A
Twitter! Tweet! Squawk!

My Favorite Place in Hong Kong

by Caren B. Stelson
Leveled Reader 84A
Genre: Photo Essay
Level: Easy

Summary

A young boy uses words and pictures to take readers on a tour of his hometown—Hong Kong. Readers learn where Hong Kong is and see photos of its harbor and busy streets. Then they visit the boy's favorite place, the Bird Market. Through their tour of this colorful and musical market, readers learn a lot about life in Hong Kong.

At a Glance

Links to the Student Edition

✎ **Comprehension Skill:** Author's Purpose

Selection Vocabulary: *magic, learning*

Program Theme: Journeys in Time and Space
Unit Theme: Are We There Yet?

A visit to the Hong Kong Bird Market takes readers on a journey to a fascinating place.

Before Reading

Motivating the Reader
Build Background About Markets

Help students name and describe some typical shops in your community, for example, places where food, clothing, and objects for the home can be purchased. Discuss what these shops look like. Ask whether they are small or large, busy or quiet, in a mall or on a street. Explain that in some places markets are outdoors in public spaces. Ask students to share any experiences with open-air markets. Then help them role-play being shopkeepers and customers at a street market.

Preview and Predict

Have students scan the cover, text, and photographs to get an idea of what the book is about. Ask them to read the title and subtitle. Have them read the text and study the pictures on pages 2–3. Then encourage students to make predictions about the book and the kind of information it will contain. Explain that a photo essay uses pictures to give readers a lot of information. Urge students to study the photographs carefully as they read. Suggest students read to find out what the narrator's favorite place is in Hong Kong.

Point out selection vocabulary and any unfamiliar words, such as *smack, crowded, bamboo,* and *chopsticks,* that might be important to understanding the book.

During Reading

Guiding Comprehension

Use the following questions to support students as they read.

- **Page 2** What word could you use to replace *smack* that makes sense in this sentence? (right, directly)

- **Pages 2–3** Look at this picture. What does it show? How does the small map help you understand the information better? (The picture shows the city of Hong Kong. The map helps readers understand where Hong Kong is located within China.)

- **Pages 4–5** Which picture do you think shows the harbor? Why do you think so? (The picture on the far left shows the harbor. The text says the harbor has big boats, and this picture shows a big boat.)

- **Pages 6–7** Look at the words *Twitter, Tweet,* and *Squawk.* What do they mean? (They are the sounds made by birds.)

- **Pages 8–9** What is one reason birds are good pets for Hong Kong? (Birds are small and can fit in crowded Hong Kong homes.)

- **Page 9** What is more important to a Hong Kong bird owner—what a bird looks like or how it sounds? How do you know? (It is more important how the bird sounds since people in Hong Kong think the bird with the sweetest song is the best bird to have.)

- **Pages 10–13** What else besides birds can you buy at the Bird Market? (You can buy grasshoppers and crickets to feed your bird. You can also buy bird cages.)

- **Page 14** The narrator says the market "always works its magic." Does the market really use magic? (No. The market doesn't really use magic. But it is a special place that always makes the boy feel happy.)

- **Page 16** Why do you think the author wrote this book? (to teach readers about the Bird Market in Hong Kong)

Reading Strategies

If... a student uses the photos and the text to gain better understanding,	**Then...** congratulate him or her for recognizing the photo essay format.
If... a student has difficulty explaining why the author may have written the book,	**Then...** use **Model Your Thinking** below.

Model Your Thinking

Think ALOUD

🎯 **Comprehension Skill: Author's Purpose**

Authors have different reasons, or purposes, for writing books. Authors may want to express or describe something to give the reader a feeling about it. Authors may also wish to share interesting information or tell an interesting story. Good readers try to figure out the author's purposes for writing so that they can better understand the text and adjust the way they read to fit the purpose of the text. For example, when I read pages 2 through 5, I learn some important facts about Hong Kong. These clues tell me that one reason this author is writing is to inform, or tell, me something about the city. I will read this kind of book more slowly and carefully so I can make sure I understand all of its information about Hong Kong.

After Reading

Revisiting the Text

Comprehension Have pairs reread the book and use Web 1 on page 132 to list interesting story details. Have pairs use their webs to decide why the author wrote this book. Invite students to share and support their ideas. Point out that authors may have more than one purpose for writing a book.

84B

Cave Treasure

by Dona R. McDuff
Leveled Reader 84B
Genre: Informational Article
Level: Easy/Average

Summary

Sometimes treasure comes to us in the form of information. The cave paintings found in 1940 in Lascaux, France, tell scientists important information about the way people lived in the Ice Age. These paintings, which are around 17,000 years old, were found by some French school boys out exploring.

At a Glance

Links to the Student Edition

⌖ **Comprehension Skill:** Author's Purpose

Selection Vocabulary: *alphabet, newspaper, tales, cabin*

Program Theme: Journeys in Time and Space
Unit Theme: Are We There Yet?

Even simple journeys can lead to incredible discoveries, such as ancient cave paintings.

Before Reading

Motivating the Reader
Build Background About Studying History

Show students objects or photographs of objects from earlier in this century, for example a horse-drawn carriage, quill pen, wind-up clock or watch, or article of clothing. Help students use these items to draw conclusions about the way people lived in an earlier time. Then explain that scientists also find out about the past by studying objects. They look at the materials and tools people used long-ago and at the pictures they drew to understand the lives these people led.

Preview and Predict

Have students scan the cover, text, and illustrations to get an idea of what the book is about. Encourage students to make predictions about what the cave treasure might be and how it is discovered. Suggest students read to find out if their predictions are correct, revising them as needed.

Point out selection vocabulary and any unfamiliar words, such as *passage, cave, mold,* and *chamber,* that might be important to understanding the book.

During Reading

Guiding Comprehension

Use the following questions to support students as they read.

- **Pages 2–3** *When and where does this book take place?* (It takes place in 1940 in Lascaux, France.)

- **Pages 6–7** *What do Marcel and his friends discover?* (They find a cave filled with many paintings.)

- **Page 8** *How do think the boys know they have found something special?* (They think the paintings are very beautiful. They have never seen anything else like these paintings.)

- **Page 10** *Look at the sentence: "The newspaper carries a story." What does this mean? Restate the sentence in your own words.* (The newspaper printed a news story about the caves.)

- **Pages 10–11** *What happened to the caves in the years after they were discovered?* (Many people came to visit, with a short break for WWII.) *What problem did visitors to the cave cause? How was the problem solved?* (People's warm breath caused mold to grow. The mold began to destroy the paintings, so the caves were closed to the public. Only scientists are allowed to view the paintings now.)

- **Page 13** *What does the table show you?* (It shows how many drawings were found of the listed animals.) *Which animal was painted most often?* (the horse)

- **Pages 14–15** *What have scientists learned from studying the Lascaux cave paintings? What would they like to learn?* (They learned the sizes of the caves, the types of paintings, and the age of the paintings. They still want to know what the dots and lines mean and why the artists painted these pictures.)

- **Page 16** *Why do you think the author wrote this book?* (to tell readers about an important discovery)

Ongoing Assessment

Reading Strategies

If... a student can summarize information,	Then... praise him or her for focusing on and remembering important ideas.
If... a student confuses the meanings of *carries* on page 10,	Then... help him or her find context clues to figure out the correct meaning.
If... a student has difficulty explaining why the author may have written the book,	Then... use **Model Your Thinking** below.

Model Your Thinking

 **Comprehension Skill: Author's Purpose**

 Think ALOUD

An author's purpose is the reason why an author writes something. Authors write for different reasons. They might want to share information with you, make you laugh or cry, describe a special moment, or convince you to agree with them. Thinking about why an author writes something helps me decide how to read. I read more slowly when a book contains a lot of information. I read more quickly when I am reading something entertaining. This book contains mostly facts about the discovery of cave paintings in France in 1940. I think one reason why the author wrote this book was to inform me about this discovery. I know I should read slowly and carefully to be sure I understand all the information.

After Reading

Revisiting the Text

Comprehension Use Web 1 on page 132. Have pairs write the author's purpose or purposes in the center of the web and list details that support their answer at the ends of the web's spokes. Then have partners take turns role-playing an interview between the author and a newspaper reporter.

85A
Junior

by Steve Otfinoski
Leveled Reader 85A
Genre: Tall Tale
Level: Easy

Summary

When Pecos Bill, the legendary cowboy, gets a cold, his son Junior steps in to drive the cattle to market. Junior's trip is full of adventures. When Junior gets hungry, he turns a cornfield into popcorn. When he gets thirsty, he drinks the lake dry. When cattle thieves try to take Junior's cattle, he leaves the men stranded in a huge dust storm. Junior shows he and his famous father have a lot in common.

At a Glance

Links to the Student Edition

✑ **Comprehension Skill:** Plot

Selection Vocabulary: *pony, dust*

Program Theme: Journeys in Time and Space
Unit Theme: Are We There Yet?

Journeys can be both surprising and funny, even when they include some scary moments.

Before Reading

Motivating the Reader
Build Background About Exaggeration

Write these sentences on the chalkboard: *He was so thirsty that he drank an entire glass of water. He was so thirsty that he drank an entire swimming pool.* Have students decide which sentence is an exaggeration—something that stretches the truth beyond what is real. Give students sentence starters, such as *She sneezed so hard that . . . .* Invite them to complete these sentences using exaggeration. Students can draw pictures illustrating their favorite exaggeration. Encourage students to think about exaggeration as they read the tall tale *Junior.*

Preview and Predict

Have students scan the cover, text, and illustrations to get an idea of what the book is about. Ask them to read the title and predict which character in the cover illustration is Junior. Prepare students to read by drawing their attention to the western setting and cartoon style of the illustrations. Then have them predict the tone—serious, funny, scary—this book might have. Suggest students read to find out who Junior is and what happens to him.

Point out selection vocabulary and any unfamiliar words, such as *cowboy, cattle, magnifying glass,* and *critters,* that might be important to understanding the book.

During Reading

Guiding Comprehension

Use the following questions to support students as they read.

- **Page 3** Look at the word *frisky*. What do you think it means? What other word in the same sentence helps you tell? (It means "playful." The word *fun-loving* is a clue.)

- **Page 4** What happens when Bill sneezed? Do you think this really could really happen? (The story says the sneeze blew the roof off the house. No. It is exaggerated in order to create humor.)

- **Pages 6–7** How does Junior get food for himself and the cattle? (He uses a magnifying glass to pop corn from a cornfield.)

- **Page 8** What happens at the lake? (Junior is so thirsty he and the animals drink all the water in the lake, and the land becomes a desert.)

- **Page 9** Is Junior like other boys you know? Why or why not? (No. He can do things that aren't possible in real life, such as turn a field of corn into popcorn.)

- **Page 12** Why do you think the men laugh loudly? (They were worried that Pecos Bill would stop them from stealing the cattle. They laugh at Junior because they think a little boy won't be able to stop them.)

- **Page 13** What do you think will happen next? (Predictions may vary, but should indicate that Junior will save the cattle from the cattle thieves.)

- **Pages 14–15** How does Junior get the cattle away safely? (He and Sugarfoot move the cattle so quickly it creates a dust cloud. The men can't see through the dust cloud, and Junior escapes with the cattle.)

- **Page 16** How does the story end? (Junior delivers the cattle and returns to the ranch. His father is proud of the way Junior tricked the cattle thieves.)

Ongoing Assessment

Reading Strategies

If... a student reads the exaggerations in a light-hearted tone,	Then... congratulate him or her for recognizing the humor.
If... a student stumbles over the word *critters* on page 13,	Then... ask him or her to think of another word that would make sense in the sentence.
If... a student has difficulty describing the book's plot,	Then... use **Model Your Thinking** below.

Model Your Thinking

Think **ALOUD**

Comprehension Skill: Plot

A story's plot includes the important events that happen in the beginning, middle, and end of the story. As I read, I look for important events that keep the story going. For example, in the beginning of this story, Pecos Bill lets Junior take the cattle to the market. The middle of the story is all about Junior's adventures getting the cattle to the market. The story ends with Junior returning to his proud papa. Good readers keep track of the important events in the beginning, middle, and end of the story because it helps them predict what might happen next. It also helps them remember and retell the story later.

After Reading

Revisiting the Text

Comprehension Have pairs reread the book and record plot events in the Plot/Story Sequence organizer on page 137. Pairs can then use their organizers to present dramatic retellings of different story events, using gesture and tone of voice to convey the story's humor.

85B

My Dog Dusty

by Nat Gabriel
Leveled Reader 85B
Genre: Historical Fiction
Level: Easy/Average

Summary

As a dust storm hurtles toward Toby's Oklahoma farm, he and his mother struggle to protect the house from the storm's damage. Then Toby hears a dog barking outside. Despite the danger, Toby races outside to rescue the dog. Mother and son smile at Dusty, the one good thing to come out of the dust storm.

At a Glance

Links to the Student Edition

☞ **Comprehension Skill:** Plot

Selection Vocabulary: *dust, pasture, chores, swift, sturdy, saddle*

**Program Theme: Journeys in Time and Space
Unit Theme: Are We There Yet?**

Some journeys are very important to make, because they let us help others.

Before Reading

Motivating the Reader
Build Background About Dust Storms

Ask a volunteer to locate Oklahoma on a class map. Invite volunteers to share any knowledge of the state's geography and climate. Explain that Oklahoma and other surrounding prairie states sometimes experience strong winds that pick up dry soil and create a storm of dust. During the 1930s, when this story takes place, there were so many dust storms in this region that it was called the Dust Bowl. Many farms were ruined by the dust, forcing people to leave the area.

Preview and Predict

Have students scan the cover, text, and illustrations to get an idea of what the book is about. Draw students' attention to the story setting described on page 2 and ask them to use the background information you have provided to make predictions about what might happen in the story. Students can set their own purpose for reading, such as reading to find out more about the relationship between the boy and his dog Dusty.

Point out selection vocabulary and any unfamiliar words, such as *gritty* and *drifts,* that might be important to understanding the book.

During Reading

Guiding Comprehension

Use the following questions to support students as they read.

- **Pages 2–3** *When and where does this story take place?* (It takes place in Oklahoma in 1935.) *What causes Toby to wake up?* (He hears the sound of a dust storm coming.)

- **Pages 4–5** *How do you think the dust has gotten into Toby's hair and mouth and ears? How will wet rags help keep it out of the house?* (The wind blows dust through the gaps in the windows and walls. Wet rags help close up the gaps and catch the dust.)

- **Pages 6–7** *What does the fluffy line around Toby mean in this picture? Why does the large picture show a green field?* (The line means that Toby is thinking or daydreaming. The large picture shows his daydream of what the field looked like before the dust came.)

- **Page 8** *What does swift mean? How do you know?* (It means "quick." The word *ran* is a clue.)

- **Page 10** *What does Toby hear?* (He hears a dog barking.) *What could happen to the dog if it is caught out in the storm?* (It could be injured or killed.)

- **Page 12** *Why does Toby think his mother will be mad? Do you think she will be mad?* (He thinks she will be mad because he goes out into the storm. She will probably be more worried about Toby's safety than mad.)

- **Pages 14–15** *How do you think the storm makes Toby feel? Why is it so important to him to save the dog?* (The dust storms have ruined the farm and made Toby feel helpless. Saving the dog makes him feel as if he can still do some good.)

- **Page 16** *How does the story end?* (After a few months, the dust is almost gone. Toby and Dusty play together happily in the green fields.)

Reading Strategies

If... a student cannot visualize a dust storm,	**Then...** use illustrations from the story or other sources to clarify how destructive such storms can be.
If... a student has trouble describing the book's plot,	**Then...** use **Model Your Thinking** below.

Model Your Thinking

 Comprehension Skill: Plot

 Think ALOUD

A story's plot includes the most important events that happen in the beginning, middle, and end of the story. Good readers keep track of these story events and try to notice which events belong in the beginning, middle, and end. In the beginning of the story, Toby and his mother are getting ready for the dust storm that is coming. The middle of the story is all about Toby's rescue of a dog he names Dusty. The story ends months later with Toby and Dusty playing in green fields that are almost clear of the dust.

After Reading

Revisiting the Text

Comprehension Have pairs reread the book and record important story events in the Plot/Story Sequence organizer on page 137. Have them draw a picture for each box in the organizer. Pairs can then use their organizers and pictures to retell the story to other pairs.

86A
The Lesson

by Judy Nayer
Leveled Reader 86A
Genre: Play
Level: Easy

Summary

A piñata maker and his wife live in a small Mexican village. They have little money, but the piñata maker loves his work. One day a rich man pays so much money for a piñata that the piñata maker no longer has to work. Not working, however, makes the piñata maker bored and unhappy, so he quickly returns to the work he loves.

At a Glance

Links to the Student Edition

☞ **Comprehension Skill:** Steps in a Process

Selection Vocabulary: *creating, designed, paste, swan, famous*

Program Theme: Creativity
Unit Theme: Imagination.kids

Creating beautiful objects that bring joy can also bring great satisfaction to the creator.

Before Reading

Motivating the Reader
Build Background About Piñatas

If you can, show and let students handle a real piñata. Break it open so students can see its construction. Alternatively, show pictures of piñatas and relate the construction process to papier mâché. Then give students materials with which to build a simple dome using papier mâché over a ball or balloon.

Preview and Predict

Have students scan the cover, text, and illustrations to get an idea of what the book is about. Point out and clarify the dramatic format. Help students use the illustrations to identify the various characters. Ask them to read the title and predict which character will learn a lesson and what that lesson might be. Suggest students read to find out if their predictions are correct.

Point out selection vocabulary and any unfamiliar words, such as *piñata* and *blindfolded,* that might be important to understanding the book.

During Reading

Guiding Comprehension

Use the following questions to support students as they read.

- **Pages 2–3** Look at this list of players. Who are these people? How can you tell who is speaking in the play? (They are the characters in the play. Each one's name appears before his or her words.)

- **Page 3** How does the piñata maker feel about his work? How do you know? (He loves it. He says he can't wait to start work.)

- **Page 4** What do the children want? (They want the piñata maker to show them how to make a piñata.)

- **Page 6** What did the piñata maker do before he put out the materials? (He cut out cardboard wings and a beak.) What kind of piñata do you think he will make? Why? (Since birds have wings and a beak, he will probably make some kind of bird.)

- **Page 6** What does the piñata maker do before he can paste newspaper on the pot? (First he has to make paste by adding water to flour.)

- **Pages 8–9** How do you think the rich man's daughter feels when she sees the piñata being made? (She feels happy and excited. She wants to watch and learn about making piñatas.)

- **Pages 11–12** What happens to the swan piñata? (The piñata maker fills it with candy and gives it to the rich man's daughter to break open with a stick.)

- **Pages 13–14** What does the rich man give the piñata maker? (money) What does the piñata maker do after he is paid? Why? (The piñata maker stops working because he now has a lot of money.)

- **Pages 15–16** How does the piñata maker feel when he stops working? What lesson does he learn? (He's bored and unhappy. He realizes creating piñatas matters more to him than money.)

Ongoing Assessment

Reading Strategies

If... a student has difficulty telling which character is speaking,	**Then...** point out the use of character names before dialogue.
If... a student confuses the italicized stage directions in parentheses for dialogue,	**Then...** ask him or her to identify who is talking and look again at what that person has said.
If... a student has difficulty following steps in a process,	**Then...** use **Model Your Thinking** below.

Model Your Thinking

Comprehension Skill: Steps in a Process

Think ALOUD

This book is about making piñatas, a process which takes many steps. When reading about how something is made, it is important to understand the order of the steps. As I read, I look for clue words such as *first, next, then,* and *later* that hint at the order of the steps. For example, on page 6 of this book, the piñata maker says that *first* he will add water, *next* he will paste newspaper, and *then* he will paste wings and a beak onto the body. Thinking about the order of these steps helps me better understand how to make a piñata.

After Reading

Revisiting the Text

Comprehension Ask students if they can picture how a piñata is made. Have them reread pages 6, 7, and 11 and help them use the Steps in a Process organizer on page 148 to record the steps in making a piñata. Have them write or draw each step in one of the boxes. You may need to add extra boxes to include drying the piñata and filling it with candy.

86B
Super Paper Snakes

by Susan Blackaby
Leveled Reader 86B
Genre: How-To Article
Level: Easy/Average

Summary

Snakes are slippery and slimy, right? Not necessarily. This book tells readers how to construct their own personalized papier-mâché snakes. Step-by-step instructions and five "Slick Tricks" guide snake makers from start to finish.

At a Glance

Links to the Student Edition

Comprehension Skill: Steps in a Process

Selection Vocabulary: *cone, creating*

Program Theme: Creativity
Unit Theme: Imagination.kids

If you follow steps correctly, you can make something interesting and fun like papier-mâché snakes.

Before Reading

Motivating the Reader
Build Background About Creativity

Show students some photographs of real snakes. Work together to describe the different snakes, and list students' descriptions on the chalkboard. Then ask volunteers to draw snakes on the chalkboard. Discuss the drawings, emphasizing the creative differences that are the result of each artist's imagination.

Preview and Predict

Have students scan the cover, text, and illustrations to get an idea of what the book is about. Ask them to read the title and first two sentences of the book before making a prediction about the book's topic. Point out the list of materials on page 3 and the speech balloons throughout. Have students read one of the puns in the speech balloons and tell how it is related to the rest of the text on the page. Suggest students read to find out how to make paper snakes.

Point out selection vocabulary and any unfamiliar words, such as *materials* and *slick,* that might be important to understanding the book. Encourage students to look for ways the dialogue in the speech balloons uses word play to make jokes about different steps.

During Reading

Guiding Comprehension

Use the following questions to support students as they read.

- **Pages 2–3** What do the words in the list the snake is holding tell you? (The list shows the materials needed to make paper snakes.)

- **Page 4** What do the words in the speech balloons mean? How do they add to the main text on the page? (It is a word play on *wire-why are*. It's just for fun. The main text has all the necessary information about the first step.)

- **Pages 4–5** How are the first step and Slick Trick Number 1 related? (The trick is a helpful tip about how to do the step. The first step is to get a piece of wire. The trick suggests leaving room at both ends of the wire that can be used later.)

- **Page 7** Do you think it would be a good idea to make a paper snake that is thirty feet long? Why or why not? (No. It would take too long and be difficult to make a paper snake thirty feet long.)

- **Page 8** How could you use newspaper padding to change your snake's shape? (You could put extra newspaper in some places to build up bumps like a head.)

- **Pages 10–11** How is the newspaper added in this step different from the newspaper used on pages 6–7? (It is torn in strips and dipped in glue. The first newspaper was in a sheet and simply wrapped around the wire.)

- **Page 13** How is a cone used to help you make a paper snake? (You can use a cone to help give your paper snake a coil. It makes the snake look more real.)

- **Pages 14–15** Will your snake look the same or different from someone else's snake if you both follow these steps? Explain. (Each person's snake will look different because you choose the length, shape, curves, and decide how to decorate it.)

Ongoing Assessment

Reading Strategies

If... a student stumbles over the speech balloon text,	**Then...** urge him or her to skip these until completing the entire main book text.
If... a student finds the direction text confusing,	**Then...** have him or her use the illustrations to see how the step should be done.
If... a student has difficulty following steps in a process,	**Then...** use **Model Your Thinking** below.

Model Your Thinking

Think ALOUD

Ⓖ **Comprehension Skill: Steps in a Process**

Steps in a process are the steps you follow in a certain order to make or do something. This book tells how to make paper snakes. When reading how-to books like this one, I make sure I understand each step and the order of the steps. I look for clues to figure out the order of the steps. For example, the word *first* on page 4 helps me figure out the order of the steps. Numbered steps, such as "Slick Trick Number 1" on page 5, also help me figure out the order of the steps. I can also study the pictures to see how my snake should look as I do each step. By reading and following steps carefully, I can make a great paper snake.

After Reading

Revisiting the Text

Comprehension Have groups reread the book and record each step on an index card. Repeat the process with the five Slick Tricks. Have each group mix its cards and exchange them with another group. Groups can then sort and arrange the cards in order, with each Slick Trick linked to the correct step.

87A
Ana's Gift

by Sharon Fear
Leveled Reader 87A
Genre: Realistic Fiction
Level: Easy

Summary

For her grandparents' anniversary, Ana wants to send them on a visit to their old village. Unfortunately, she doesn't have enough money. She creates instead a beautiful mural that tells her grandparents' story and lets them visit their village through her art.

At a Glance

Links to the Student Edition

◎ **Comprehension Skill:** Setting

Selection Vocabulary: *bundled, conductor, station*

Program Theme: Creativity
Unit Theme: Imagination.kids

Art can be the greatest gift of all. Through art, we can bring whole worlds to life and show our love for others.

Before Reading

Motivating the Reader
Build Background About Moving

Ask volunteers to name countries other than the United States. Work together to find these on a world map. Set up a place in the room as the United States. Tell students to choose a few important objects from their desks or bookbags. Have them bring these objects when they "immigrate" to the United States. Talk about the choices they made and the problems that might arise in making such a move. Ask them to consider how these choices and problems might make good stories to tell their children and grandchildren.

Preview and Predict

Have students scan the cover, text, and illustrations to get an idea of what the book is about and how the characters are related. Have students use word and picture clues to help them make predictions about what Ana's gift is and who will receive the gift. Suggest students read to find out if their predictions are correct, revising them as needed.

Point out selection vocabulary and any unfamiliar words, such as *Abuelo, Abuela,* and *anniversary,* that might be important to understanding the book. If you have Spanish-speaking students in the class, invite them to model how to pronounce the characters' names.

During Reading

Guiding Comprehension

Use the following questions to support students as they read.

- **Pages 2–3** Who are the people in the picture? (Ana and her grandparents) **What is the grandparents' story about?** (They are telling about the town where they were born and got married.)

- **Page 4** How did Ana's grandparents get to this country? (They took a train and a boat.)

- **Pages 5–6** Why are Ana's parents having a party? (They are celebrating the fortieth wedding anniversary of Ana's grandparents.) **What gift does Ana want to give her grandparents?** (She wants to send them on a trip back to their little town.) **How do Ana's parents react to this idea?** (They say there isn't enough money for the trip.)

- **Page 8** What do you think Ana's gift will be? (Predictions may vary. Students may use picture clues to predict that it is a drawing.)

- **Pages 9–11** What does Ana's gift show? **Where did Abuelo and Abuela go on their journey?** (Ana's picture shows Ana's grandparents' story of their journey from their village to Texas.)

- **Page 13** How is Ana's father related to the baby in Ana's drawing? (They are the same person at different ages.)

- **Pages 14–15** How does Ana's gift make everyone feel? How does she feel about it? (Ana's art brings great joy to all, even Ana.)

Reading Strategies

If... a student correctly grasps that the pictures on Ana's mural show different places and time periods,	**Then...** recognize his or her ability to analyze setting.
If... a student has difficulty understanding the tone of the dialogue,	**Then...** talk about how people feel at a party or when celebrating.
If... a student has difficulty identifying the book's setting,	**Then...** use **Model Your Thinking** below.

Model Your Thinking

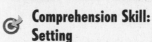 **Comprehension Skill: Setting**

Think ALOUD

A story's setting is when and where the story takes place. Sometimes authors tell us a lot about that time and place. Sometimes we have to figure out the time and place from details in the words and pictures. Some stories, like this one, describe more than one time and place. One time and place of the story is Ana's house around the time of her grandparents' wedding anniversary. The words and picture on page 5 help me figure this out. Another important time and place in the book is the journey Ana's grandparents took from their village to Texas before Ana's father was born. The words and pictures on pages 9–12 help me figure out what this journey was like.

After Reading

Revisiting the Text

Comprehension Have students reread the book and use the T-Chart on page 150 to describe the two settings of the story—long ago and now. They can list time and place details for long ago on the left and similar details about now on the right. Have students then tell what happens in each setting.

87B

The Best Place of All

by Gloria Dominic
Leveled Reader 87B
Genre: Realistic Story
Level: Easy/Average

Summary

Juan sells bus tickets in a busy city bus station. Every day he watches people begin trips to new places. Juan dreams of one day going on his own journey to see the world's excitements. When the bus company gives him a free trip, Juan gets a chance to make his dream come true.

At a Glance

Links to the Student Edition

☞ **Comprehension Skill:** Setting

Selection Vocabulary: *carted, label, mailing*

Program Theme: Creativity
Unit Theme: Imagination.kids

Imagination can open the doors to many new experiences, but sometimes those experiences turn out to be different than what we imagine.

Before Reading

Motivating the Reader
Build Background About Travel and Vacations

Bring in travel photographs or brochures. Invite students to share experiences of journeys they have taken or dreams of trips they would like to take. Have them draw places—real or imagined—that they would like to visit. Work together to create a classroom bulletin board of travel experiences and dreams of traveling.

Preview and Predict

Have students scan the cover, text, and illustrations to get an idea of what the book is about. Invite a volunteer to read the title aloud and then ask students to predict where the best place of all will be. Students can read to find out if their predictions are correct. Remind them they can revise their predictions as they read new information.

Point out selection vocabulary and any unfamiliar words, such as *schedules* and *honeymoon,* that might be important to understanding the book. Explain that *Amigo* means "friend" in Spanish.

During Reading

Guiding Comprehension

Use the following questions to support students as they read.

- **Pages 2–3** Look at this picture. Why does Juan have a picture of a far-away place on his wall and boats on his bed covers? What do these clues tell you about him? (He likes to think about far-away places and travel.)

- **Pages 2–3** What kind of place does Juan dream about? (He dreams of a warm place with a pool and palm trees at sunset.)

- **Pages 4–5** How is the place where Juan lives different from the place where he works? (He lives in a house outside the city, but he works at a bus station in a crowded city neighborhood.)

- **Page 6** Look at the word OPEN in the text and illustration. What does *open* mean in this context? (The ticket counter is open, or ready, for business.)

- **Pages 6–7** What kind of job does Juan have? (He works at a bus station selling bus tickets and helping travelers figure out the best way to travel.)

- **Pages 8–9** What does Juan think about all the travelers? (He thinks they will have happy times in interesting places.)

- **Pages 10–11** What does the bus company give Juan? How does it change his life? (They give him a bus ticket to go wherever he wants to go. He gets to take his dream trip.)

- **Pages 12–13** What is the place Juan visits like? How is it like the place he dreamed of visiting? (It is a warm, sunny, beach place that is just like Juan's dream place.)

- **Pages 14–15** How does Juan feel about his vacation and about his home? (He enjoys his vacation, but he misses his home.)

- **Page 16** What lesson does Juan learn? (It is fun to visit new places, but home is the best place of all.)

Model Your Thinking

 Comprehension Skill: Setting

 Think ALOUD

A story's setting is when and where the story takes place. In this book, Juan works in a busy bus station, but he dreams of visiting other places. As I read, I look for details about where and when the story takes place and whether that time or place changes at all. I also think about whether the setting affects what characters feel or do. In this story, Juan visits a place he's only dreamt about. On page 12, he compares its setting to the way he'd imagined it in his dream on page 2. Because the two settings are so much the same, Juan feels happy. However, Juan soon misses his home and his friends at the bus station. He learns that, while new places are fun to visit, home is the best place to be.

After Reading

Revisiting the Text

Comprehension Have pairs reread the book and draw three pictures of Juan—at home, at work, and on vacation. Have students write a caption for each picture to describe the setting and how Juan feels about each place.

88A
The Sandwich Queen

by Sydnie Meltzer Kleinhenz
Leveled Reader 88A
Genre: Realistic Story
Level: Easy

Summary

Vera's mom accidentally packs Vera a very unusual sandwich of peanut butter and pickles. The other students are fascinated by the creative sandwich. Vera is pleased by this attention and begins to explore even more creative sandwich combinations with some surprising results!

At a Glance

Links to the Student Edition

☞ **Comprehension Skill:** Visualizing

Selection Vocabulary: *flushed, hurled, pronounced, sauce, success*

Program Theme: Creativity
Unit Theme: Imagination.kids

Creative ideas can make even the most ordinary parts of life more fun and interesting—they can also help people enjoy one another.

Before Reading

Motivating the Reader
Build Background About Shyness

Ask for volunteers to role-play a bus ride. Gather two or more students in one part of the room, place a single student a short distance away from the other group of students. Instruct the single student to be a very shy character. The others are all good friends. Have the volunteers act out a scene that shows how the shy person and the group of friends would act toward one another. Encourage students to discuss the shy character's experience and emotions and to think about the challenges of shyness as they read the book.

Preview and Predict

Have students scan the cover, text, and illustrations to get an idea of what the book is about. Draw students' attention to the expressions on characters' faces throughout the book. Encourage them to make predictions about the characters' emotions and how these might relate to the main events of the story. Suggest students read to find out who and what a sandwich queen is.

Point out selection vocabulary and any unfamiliar words, such as *creative* and *outrageous,* that might be important to understanding the book. Discuss the use of word play in knock-knock jokes.

During Reading

Guiding Comprehension

Use the following questions to support students as they read.

- **Page 2** How do you think Vera's mom feels? How do you know? (Vera's mom feels hurried and stressed. The words and the picture show that she is trying to work fast because she is late.)

- **Page 3** How does Vera feel? How do you know? (She doesn't feel comfortable around the other kids. The picture shows her frowning and sitting by herself. The other kids call her "Vera Shy.")

- **Pages 4–5** What mistake did Vera's mom make? (She mixed up the ingredients on the sandwiches and gave Vera a peanut butter and pickle sandwich.) How does this mistake become a success? (The other students notice Vera's surprised reaction to the sandwich. They think the sandwich and Vera are creative. The unusual sandwich gets Vera and the other students talking and laughing.)

- **Page 6** Why is Vera excited and flushed? (She's enjoying all the attention she's getting. She feels special.)

- **Page 7** How do the students use Vera's name as part of a knock-knock joke? (They say *Vera* instead of *very*.)

- **Pages 12–13** Look at the pictures and the words. How are Vera and the other kids getting along? How can you tell? (They have all become friends. The other kids are copying Vera's sandwiches and talking to her.)

- **Pages 14–15** How do you think this sandwich tastes? How do you know? (It tastes too spicy because of the hot sauce. Vera's face and neck get red after she takes a bite.)

- **Page 16** How has Vera changed by the end of the book? (She's less shy. She's learned to tell a joke.)

Ongoing Assessment

Reading Strategies

If... a student uses the proper intonation for *Outrageous!* and other exclamations,	**Then...** congratulate him or her for understanding exclamation marks and reading with expression.
If... a student has difficulty visualizing characters, setting, or events,	**Then...** use **Model Your Thinking** below.

Model Your Thinking

 Comprehension Skill: Visualizing

 Think ALOUD

Can you picture the crowded lunchroom at your school? Can you imagine what a sandwich made of peanut butter and pickles looks like? When you use your senses to create pictures in your mind about what you are reading, you are visualizing. Visualizing can help you feel like part of the story. Good readers use words from the story about how things look, sound, taste, feel, or smell to help them visualize. They also use their own experiences. For example, in this book, I can close my eyes and visualize Vera making one of her creative sandwiches. I look for details in the story about Vera and what ingredients she uses. I think about what I know about these foods and how they taste. Visualizing Vera's sandwiches helps me better understand how the characters react to them.

After Reading

Revisiting the Text

Comprehension Have students reread the book and make a list of the different sandwiches Vera makes. Have students pick a favorite and write a food review about it, using sensory details to describe it. Invite students to share their reviews.

88B
Ready to Cook

by Susan McCloskey
Leveled Reader 88B
Genre: How-To Article
Level: Easy/Average

Summary

Ready Fox tells readers about a selection of real recipes that are easy enough for children to make. He gives clear directions and safety tips. Ready Fox also suggests some new twists on old favorites like peanut butter and jelly. Mixed in with all the practical how-to tips are Ready's funny jokes.

At a Glance

Links to the Student Edition

⌖ **Comprehension Skill:** Visualizing

Selection Vocabulary: *refrigerator, sauce*

Program Theme: Creativity
Unit Theme: Imagination.kids

Cooking is a creative process where you can let your imagination lead you to tasty new treats!

Before Reading

Motivating the Reader
Build Background About Cooking

If possible, take students to visit a real kitchen. Ask kitchen workers to explain some of the tools and processes they use. Otherwise, bring in a simple selection of cooking utensils, and discuss how they are used to prepare food. Invite students to tell about some of their favorite foods, especially those special to their culture or family. Have students explain any unfamiliar foods.

Preview and Predict

Have students scan the cover, text, and illustrations to get an idea of what the book is about. Read the title aloud and point out characteristics of the how-to genre, explaining that this book contains real directions to make real foods. Help students identify Ready Fox and some of the foods he uses, and then ask them to predict what kinds of dishes he might suggest cooking. Suggest students read to find out which food they think would taste the best or be fun to make.

Point out selection vocabulary and any unfamiliar words, such as *recipe,* that might be important to understanding the book. You may also want to point out the foods named in the book as some students may not be familiar with them.

During Reading

Guiding Comprehension

Use the following questions to support students as they read.

- **Pages 2–3** *What does Ready Fox like to do?* (cook and tell jokes)

- **Page 4** *Which step do you do first to make this chicken dish?* (Put pieces of chicken in yogurt.)

- **Page 4** *What safety tips does Ready Fox give readers to keep them safe when cooking?* (He says to have a grown-up help you bake the chicken. He says wash your hands after touching raw chicken.)

- **Pages 6–7** *What does Ready Fox mean when he says "Then take a bow as you serve them!"?* (Everyone will love your mashed potatoes so much that they'll probably clap.)

- **Page 8** *What does it mean to "skip the jelly"?* (It means to leave the jelly out of the sandwich.)

- **Page 10** *What foods are in the sandwich Ready Fox suggests for taking to school?* (bread, cream cheese, and sunflower seeds or apples)

- **Page 10** *Look at the word yum. What do you think Ready Fox means?* (He means it tastes good.)

- **Pages 11–12** *Why would taking a spoon out of the cup keep your eyes from hurting?* (If you don't take the spoon out, you could poke yourself in the eye.)

- **Page 14** *What does Ready Fox suggest to make hot cereal taste good?* (Fill a well in the center of the cereal with syrup or honey.) *What does Ready Fox mean when he says to "make a little well in the center"? Use the picture to help you figure this out.* (He means to make a small hole in your cereal that can hold honey or syrup.)

- **Page 16** *Which recipe would you like to try? Why?* (Encourage well-supported answers.)

Model Your Thinking

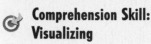 **Comprehension Skill: Visualizing**

 Think ALOUD

Visualizing means creating pictures in your mind as you read. Good readers look for words that describe how something looks, sounds, tastes, smells, or feels. They also think about what they already know about what is being described. For example, on page 14, the words *little well* help me picture a small hole in the middle of the cereal. I think about how sweet the hot cereal will taste if I add honey or syrup to the well. Visualizing helps me better understand how to make Ready Fox's recipes and how these foods might taste.

After Reading

Revisiting the Text

Comprehension Ask students which of Ready Fox's foods they'd most like to eat. Then have pairs write and illustrate a recipe card of this food. Students can use the Steps in a Process organizer to help them organize their thinking.

89A
Chasing Riley

by Donna Latham-Levine
Leveled Reader 89A
Genre: Realistic Story
Level: Easy

Summary

Jess and Tyler are out of ideas for what to do. Then Tyler's sister takes them to the duck pond where they run into Jess's neighbor Miriam. Miriam's after-school job is walking dogs. When Miriam's puppy Riley escapes to chase a giant bird, the fun begins. No one is bored anymore!

At a Glance

Links to the Student Edition

☞ **Comprehension Skill:** Plot

Selection Vocabulary: *unusual, weighed*

Program Theme: Creativity
Unit Theme: Imagination.kids

A little imagination goes a long way toward changing a dull day into an exciting adventure.

Before Reading

Motivating the Reader
Build Background About Puppies

Ask volunteers to share experiences with or knowledge of puppies. Use Web 1 on page 132 or make a word web on the chalkboard to record students' ideas. Have students list behavior characteristics they associate with puppies. Also ask them to list tasks people must perform to care for puppies and other dogs. Have students watch for these behaviors and tasks as they read the book.

Preview and Predict

Have students scan the cover, text, and illustrations to get an idea of what the book is about. Have students look at the cover illustration and title before predicting who Riley is and why he needs to be chased. Suggest students read to find out more about Riley and what he does in the book.

Point out selection vocabulary and any unfamiliar words, such as *customers, pterodactyl,* and *extinct,* that might be important to understanding the book.

During Reading

Guiding Comprehension

Use the following questions to support students as they read.

- **Pages 2–3** *Look at this picture. Which character do you think is Jess? What words and pictures tell you so?* (Jess is the boy holding the basketball. The words say "He tossed the ball up and down.") *How do Jess and Tyler feel?* (They both feel bored.)

- **Pages 6–7** *Why do Tyler, Jess, and Nikki go to the duck pond? Who do they meet there?* (They go to feed the ducks. They meet Miriam and her many dogs.)

- **Pages 7–8** *Look at the word customers. Why does Miriam call the dogs her customers?* (Miriam gets paid to walk other people's dogs.)

- **Page 8** *Who is Riley?* (Riley is a small puppy that belongs to Miriam.)

- **Pages 10–11** *Do you think Nikki has really seen a flying dinosaur? Why does she think she has?* (No. Dinosaurs are extinct, but the blue heron looks like a pterodactyl.)

- **Pages 11–14** *What does Riley do when he sees the blue heron?* (He escapes from Miriam and chases after the bird.) *What happens next?* (Miriam and the boys chase after Riley all through the park. They finally catch him when Jess stops Riley by rolling his basketball to the puppy.)

- **Pages 15–16** *How does the story end?* (Miriam decides to take Riley and the other dogs home. Jess and Tyler make plans to help Miriam walk the dogs the next day.)

- **Page 16** *How do Jess and Tyler feel about their day now?* (They had fun and realize that adventures sometimes appear unexpectedly.)

Ongoing Assessment

Reading Strategies

If...	Then...
If... a student seems confused by the reference to Follow the Leader,	**Then...** direct him or her to the illustration of the ducks for clarification.
If... a student stumbles over the word *pterodactyl* on page 10,	**Then...** model the correct pronunciation (ter′ ə dak′ təl) and have the student echo you.
If... a student has trouble describing the book's plot,	**Then...** use **Model Your Thinking** below.

Model Your Thinking

 Comprehension Skill: Plot

 Think ALOUD

Stories have a beginning, a middle, and an end. Together these parts make up the plot. As they read, good readers keep track of the important parts of the story. The beginning part includes the boys feeling bored and the trip to the duck pond. The middle part of the plot is meeting Miriam and the chase after Riley. The story ends when Jess and Tyler make plans to help Miriam walk her dogs the next day. By figuring out the important parts of the plot, I will be better able to remember and retell the story when I'm done reading.

After Reading

Revisiting the Text

Comprehension Have students reread the book and complete the Plot/Story Sequence organizer on page 137. They should list key events from the beginning, middle, and end of the story. Then have pairs choose one or two key events from each part of the story to depict in a cartoon. Have pairs take turns writing speech bubbles and drawing pictures.

89B

A Dad in Space

by Stacey Sparks
Leveled Reader 89B
Genre: Realistic Story
Level: Easy/Average

Summary

This book is written from the point of view of Shana's dad. Shana's dad creates a scrap book about his space travel adventures for his daughter. He tells her about the shuttle's main parts and what happens to them during take-off and landing. He describes how the lack of gravity affects his body and the jobs he must do.

At a Glance

Links to the Student Edition

Comprehension Skill: Plot

Selection Vocabulary: *astronaut, emergency, globe, launch*

Program Theme: Creativity
Unit Theme: Imagination.kids

Readers use their imagination to travel with characters on exciting journeys.

Before Reading

Motivating the Reader
Build Background About Space Travel

If possible, display photographs or videotaped broadcasts about recent shuttle trips. Invite students to tell as much as they can about the journey and its setting. Prompt students with questions:

> What special clothing do the astronauts wear? Where do they sit in the shuttle during take-off?

Have students record their ideas, using words or drawings, in Web 1 on page 132.

Preview and Predict

Have students scan the cover, text, and illustrations to get an idea of what the book is about. Read together page 2 of the book. Ask students to make predictions about what things Shana's dad will include in his book. Use the illustrations to clarify, if needed, the book-within-book structure of this story. Have students think about questions they would like to ask Shana's dad, and encourage them to read to look for the answers to these questions.

Point out selection vocabulary and any unfamiliar words, such as *weightless,* that might be important to understanding the book.

During Reading

Guiding Comprehension

Use the following questions to support students as they read.

- **Page 2** Look at the words on this page. Who is writing? (An astronaut is writing to his daughter Shana.) **What will this book be about?** (It will be about Shana's dad's experiences as an astronaut riding in a space shuttle.)

- **Page 5** What is gravity? How does the picture help you understand it? (It is the force that holds us on Earth. The picture shows the idea of gravity as a big hand pushing down on a person.)

- **Pages 6–7** What happens to the space shuttle and to Shana's dad by about twelve minutes after launch? (He becomes weightless.)

- **Page 8** What does this picture show? (It shows Shana's dad exercising on a tread mill.)

- **Page 9** What job does Shana's dad have to do? (He has to go outside the shuttle to get a broken satellite so they can bring it back to earth and fix it.)

- **Pages 10–11** What happens when Shana's dad tries to go outside to get the satellite? (He can't get it because the tool he needs to use fails.)

- **Page 12** How does Shana's dad finally complete his job? (While inside the shuttle, he moves a robot arm by remote control.)

- **Pages 14–16** How does Shana's dad feel about his journey in space? How does he feel about going home? (He has enjoyed the trip and is sad to leave outer space, but he is happy to go home to Shana and her mom.)

Ongoing Assessment

Reading Strategies

If...	Then...
If... a student uses proper intonation to express the book's dramatic moments,	**Then...** praise him or her for recognizing descriptive and action language.
If... a student has difficulty with the specialized space vocabulary or scientific topic,	**Then...** have the student try to paraphrase challenging sentences in his or her own words.
If... a student has trouble describing the book's plot.	**Then...** use **Model Your Thinking** below.

Model Your Thinking

 Comprehension Skill: Plot

 Think ALOUD

This book is about an astronaut's journey and his work on a space shuttle. Even though the book tells real information about what a space shuttle is like, it is told like a story. Stories have a beginning, a middle, and an end. Together, these parts make up the plot. As I read, I decide which events are important and help keep the plot moving. For example, the shuttle taking off is an important event in the beginning. The shuttle shaking during take-off is an interesting but less important detail. The middle part includes Shana's dad's two attempts to get the satellite. The story ends when Shana's dad returns home.

After Reading

Revisiting the Text

Comprehension Have students reread the book and use the Plot/Story Sequence organizer on page 137 to create a story map of important events. Ask students if they would like to travel to space. Have them find text and/or illustrations to support their views. For each reason given, ask students to tell which part of the story it comes from: beginning, middle, or end.

90A
Tina's Diary

by Robert R. O'Brien
Leveled Reader 90A
Genre: Fantasy
Level: Easy

Summary

In her diary, Tina turns her rainy day events into grand adventures. Making a snack turns into an avalanche of popcorn. A search for a pet cat becomes a dangerous trek through the jungle!

At a Glance

Links to the Student Edition

⌖ **Comprehension Skill:** Realism and Fantasy

Selection Vocabulary: *remarkable, blinding, sparkling, scout*

Program Theme: Creativity
Unit Theme: Imagination.kids

Imagination can change an everyday experience into an action-packed adventure.

Before Reading

Motivating the Reader
Build Background About Fantasy

Ask for two volunteers to role-play. Place two chairs and other ordinary classroom props side by side at the front of the room. Give partners a few minutes to think of how they can use the props to show two interesting characters having an incredible adventure. Ask watching students to comment on which actions could really happen and which actions could not really happen. For example, two people could have a conversation, but one person couldn't make the other person shrink by pointing a finger. Encourage students to think about the difference between what is make-believe and what is real as they read the book.

Preview and Predict

Have students scan the cover, text, and illustrations to get an idea of what the book is about. As students page through the book, point out and clarify the diary format and the use of thought bubbles. Invite students to make predictions about the bubbles' role in the story. Suggest students read to find out what Tina says in her diary about what happened and what students think really happened.

Point out selection vocabulary and any unfamiliar words, such as *diary* and *adventure,* that might be important to understanding the book.

During Reading

Guiding Comprehension

Use the following questions to support students as they read.

- **Pages 2–3** *Who is telling the story?* (Tina) *How is the story being told?* (Tina is writing about her experiences in a diary.)

- **Page 3** *What does the thought balloon show? What does the rest of the picture show?* (The thought balloon shows the event as Tina imagines it, while the rest of the picture shows what really happens.) *Is there really a river in the house? Explain.* (No. A few drops of rain come in through the window, but Tina imagines these drops are a raging river.) Ask similar questions for later events to make sure students understand that Tina's diary entries and the illustrations in the thought balloons are exaggerations of the events that actually happen.

- **Pages 5–9** *What happens during the Great Popcorn Flood?* (Tina doesn't follow directions when making popcorn and the popcorn overflows from the pot. Tina imagines that there is a flood of popcorn that fills the house and spills into the yard. She and her mom clean up the mess.)

- **Pages 8–9** *Look at the words HUGE and before. Why are these words shown in different sizes and kinds of letters? How do these differences change your reading?* (Both changes emphasize the words. They make readers notice the words and their message. You read them with greater emphasis.)

- **Pages 10–11** *Is Tina really a scout? Does she really get lost in the jungle? What is Tina doing?* (No. She isn't a scout and doesn't get lost in the jungle. She is searching for her cat to give it dinner.)

- **Page 14** *How is Tina's face different in the thought bubble than in the rest of the picture?* (In her fantasy Tina looks scared and really tired, but in the other part she just looks eager to eat.)

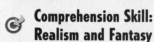
Ongoing Assessment

Reading Strategies

If... a student has difficulty telling which text refers to Tina's fantasies and which text refers to the realistic events,	**Then...** stress the contrast between the thought bubbles and the rest of the pictures.
If... a student has trouble distinguishing events that could really happen and events that could not really happen,	**Then...** use **Model Your Thinking** below.

Model Your Thinking

Think **ALOUD**

⌖ **Comprehension Skill: Realism and Fantasy**

A realistic story tells about something that could happen in real life. A fantasy has some things that could not possibly happen. It may also include things that could really happen. Good readers try to tell the difference between the two kinds of stories. I look for clues that tell me which kind of story I'm reading. For example, on page 13 of this book, Tina is riding a dragon and being chased by a giant flying bug. I know that dragons aren't real and flies don't come that big, so I know this book is a fantasy. Tina's diary entries describe things that couldn't really happen. The pictures in the book show what Tina imagines and what really happens. I have to think very carefully about the words and the pictures to decide which parts could really happen and which parts could not.

After Reading

Revisiting the Text

Comprehension Have pairs reread the book and use the T-Chart on page 150 to describe what Tina imagines and what really happens. Walk students through the book, and have volunteers tell what happens on each page.

90B
Jane in the Jungle

by Myka-Lynne Sokoloff
Leveled Reader 90B
Genre: Fantasy
Level: Easy/Average

Summary

Jane heads off to her Aunt Edna's attic in search of something interesting to do. While exploring her Aunt's treasures from a trip to Africa, Jane stumbles on some amazing instructions that, when followed, take Jane on an imaginary journey to Africa.

At a Glance

Links to the Student Edition

🎯 **Comprehension Skill:** Realism and Fantasy

Selection Vocabulary: *crystal, echoing, ledge, treasure*

Program Theme: Creativity
Unit Theme: Imagination.kids

Sometimes home seems dull, but with imagination it can be the starting point for exciting journeys.

Before Reading

Motivating the Reader
Build Background About African Wildlife

Provide books containing pictures of African animals, and assign pairs to find out about specific animals. Have partners create a flash card with the animal's name on one side and a drawing of it on the other side. Have them record on the cards details about the animals' behavior and appearance. Invite volunteers to role-play short meetings between different pairs of animals, using information from the flash cards.

Preview and Predict

Have students scan the cover, text, and illustrations to get an idea of what the book is about. Ask them to predict who Jane is and what happens to her in this story. Then open the book to page 6 and point out the boxed text. Explain that though this text is set aside, students should still read it for important information. Encourage them to look for other boxed text in this book and figure out how it relates to the main writing. Suggest students read to find out how Jane gets to the jungle and what she does in the jungle.

Point out selection vocabulary and any unfamiliar words, such as *postcard* and *instructions,* that might be important to understanding the book.

During Reading

Guiding Comprehension

Use the following questions to support students as they read.

- **Pages 2–3** What is Jane doing in her Aunt Edna's attic? (She's exploring in search of something interesting to see or do.)

- **Page 6** Why do you think the author put some writing in a box? What does the boxed writing tell Jane? (The writing is separate to show that it is what Jane reads off a piece of paper. It tells Jane how to find adventure.)

- **Page 7** What happens when Jane follows the instructions on the piece of paper? (The basket turns into a hot-air balloon, and Jane floats away.) Could this event happen in real life? Why or why not? (No. Baskets don't turn into hot-air balloons.)

- **Page 7** Where do you think Jane will go? Why? (She will go to Africa. She wrote *Africa* in the air with her nose. She is dressed for a trip to Africa.)

- **Page 8** What does the writing in this box show? (It is a postcard that Jane has written to her Aunt Edna telling her about her ride and letting her know she won't be back for lunch.)

- **Pages 10–11** How do Jane's ballet lessons help her with the lion? How do you know? (She is able to avoid the lion's charge, by twirling around. She looks like she's dancing in the picture.)

- **Pages 12–13** How does Jane feel about her adventure now? (She's had enough adventure and wants to go home.)

- **Page 16** What is the same at Aunt Edna's when Jane returns? What is different? (It is still Saturday, but Jane is no longer bored and an elephant has arrived for lunch.)

Reading Strategies

If... a student reads the boxed text throughout the book in a different tone,	**Then...** praise him or her for understanding the story structure.
If... a student has trouble distinguishing events that could really happen and events that could not really happen,	**Then...** use **Model Your Thinking** below.

Model Your Thinking

Think ALOUD

 Comprehension Skill: Realism and Fantasy

A realistic story tells about something that could happen in real life. A fantasy includes things that could not possibly happen. It may also include some things that could really happen. To tell which kind of story I am reading, I ask myself: Could this event really happen? I think about information in the story and also about my own experiences in life. For example, I know a girl could go exploring in her aunt's attic, but I also know that a basket cannot suddenly turn into a hot-air balloon. Because this story includes events that could not really happen, I know it is a fantasy.

After Reading

Revisiting the Text

Comprehension Have pairs reread the book and decide which events could really happen and which events could not really happen. Students can record their thoughts in the T-Chart on page 150. Then invite pairs to act out their favorite part of the book.

Name _____

Book Title _____

Read the title and look at the pictures in the book.
What do you think a problem in the book might be?

I think a problem might be _____

_____

_____

After reading _____ ,
draw a picture of one of the problems in the book.

Name _____

Book Title _____

Look at the book title above and the list of words and phrases below.
Write sentences that predict who and what this book might be about.

Words and Phrases

Characters: _____

_____

Problem: _____

_____

_____

_____

Events: _____

_____

_____

Outcome: _____

_____

_____

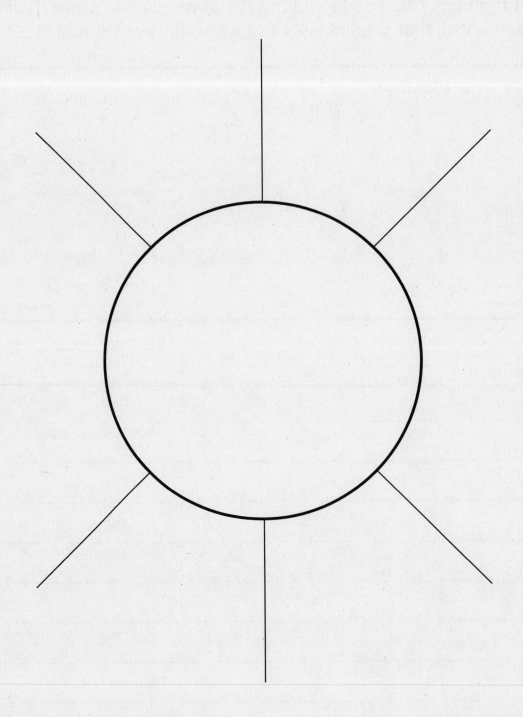

Topic

What We **K** now

What We **W** ant to Know

What We **L** earned

Name _____

[ ] **Word**

[ ] **Association or Symbol**

Predicted definition: _____

One good sentence:

_____

_____

_____

_____

Verified definition:

_____

_____

_____

Another good sentence:

_____

_____

_____

_____

Name _____

Book Title _____

Beginning

Middle

End

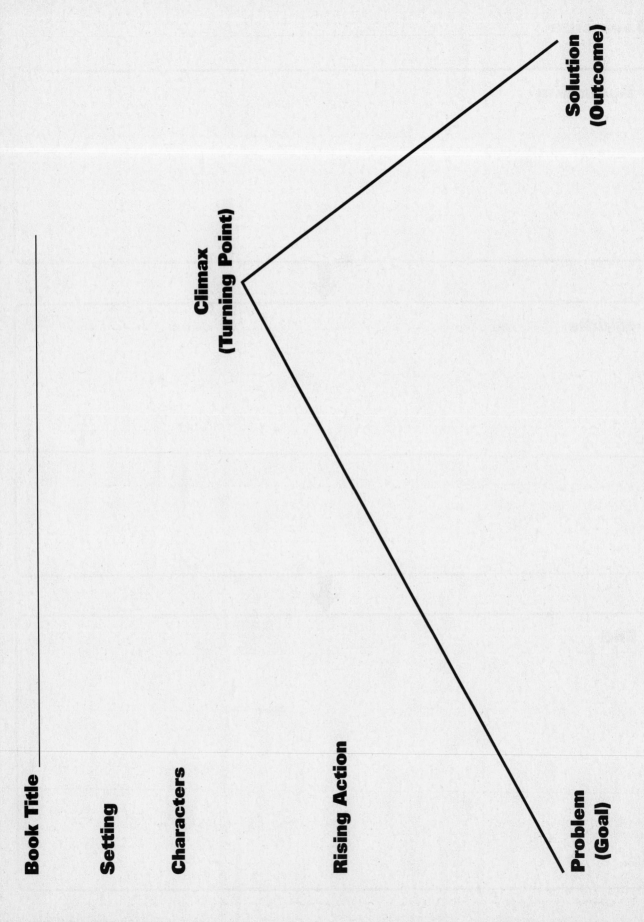

Book Title

Setting

Characters

Climax
(Turning Point)

Rising Action

Problem
(Goal)

Solution
(Outcome)

Name _____

Title

Characters

Problem

Events

_____

_____

_____

_____

_____

_____

_____

Solution

Name _____

Title A _____   **Title B** _____

_____   _____

Characters	Characters

Setting	Setting

Events	Events

Ending	Ending

Name _____

Book Title _____

Central Issues

Alike

Different

Conclusions

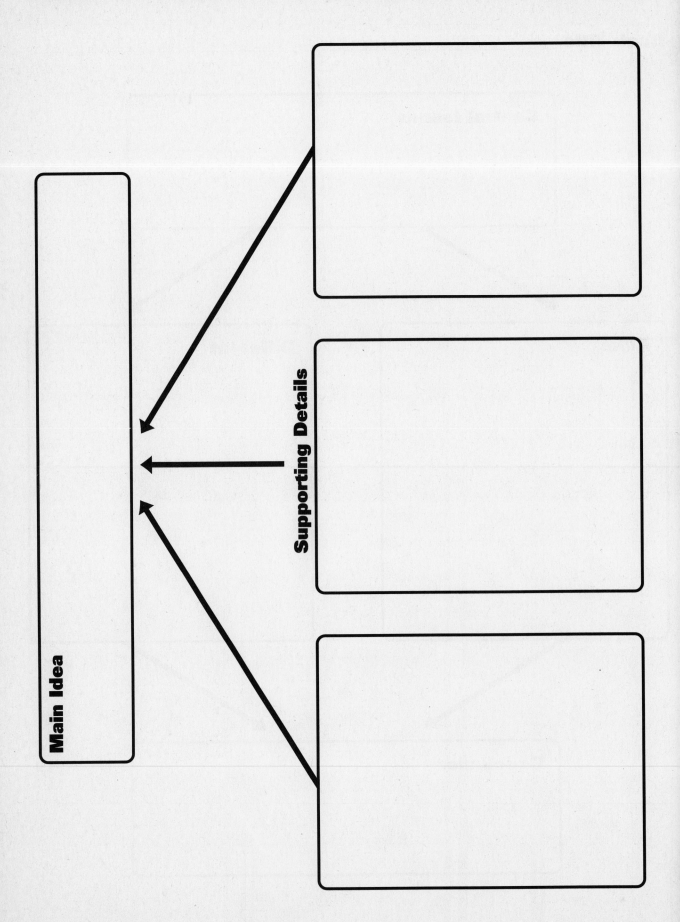

Main Idea

Supporting Details

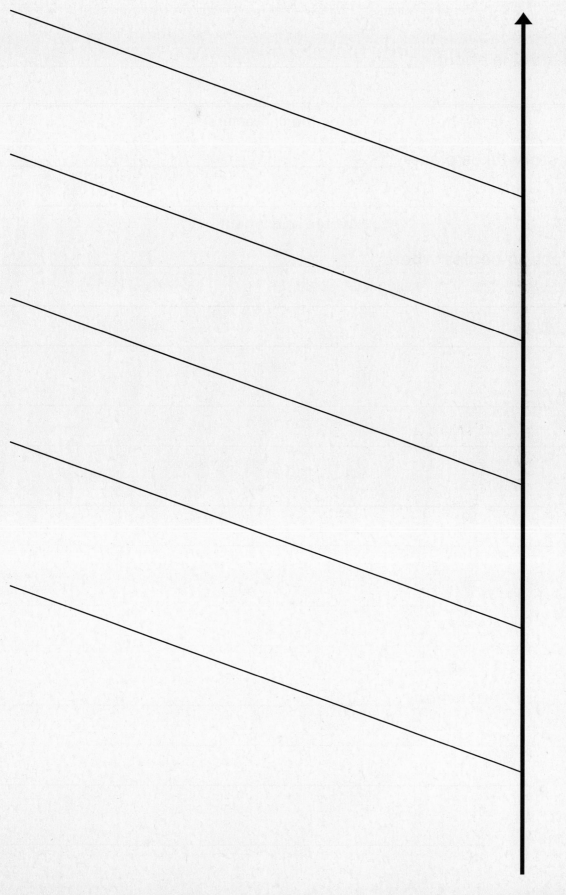

Date

Name _____

Book Title _____

This story is about _____

_____
                              (name the characters)

This story takes place _____

_____
                              (where and when)

The action begins when _____

_____

_____

Then, _____

_____

Next, _____

_____

After that, _____

_____

The story ends when _____

_____

_____

Theme: _____

Name _____

Cause

Effect

Why did it happen?

What happened?

Why did it happen?

What happened?

Why did it happen?

What happened?

Name _____

Problem

↓

Attempts to Solve the Problem

↓

Solution

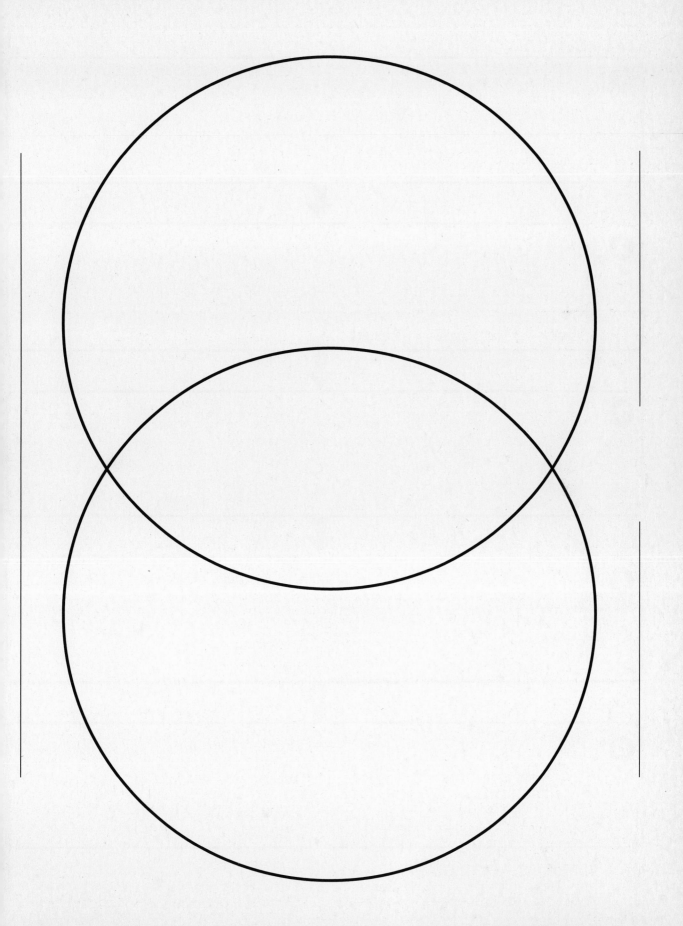

Name _____

1

2

3

4

5

Name _____

Name _____

Scott Foresman Leveling System

Stage	Language Structure	Illustrations (Art and Photos)	Vocabulary, Concepts, Content, and Genre	Text Format and Features (Book Length, Size, and Layout)	Phonics and Word Study
Beginning Independent Readers (K, 1.1)	repetitive patterns with one word substitutions, rhyme, and repetition	simple illustrations, consistent picture-to-text sequence	familiar objects and/or common experiences, many words are pictured	single line of text per page; large, clear type size and typeface; small number of words per selection	one syllable words or high frequency words predominate
Early/Novice Leveled Readers Grade 1: 1A–30A	memorable repetitive language patterns throughout, predictable forms	strong support for text, consistent picture-to-text sequence	easily understood concepts, short words	short selections with few characters; single line of text per page; large, clear type size and typeface; small number of words per selection	focus on consonants, rhyming patterns, phonograms, and phonetically regular words; greater use of high frequency words
Novice/Developing Leveled Readers Grade 1: 1B–30B Grade 2: 31A–60A	some repeated language, consistent sentence structure	pictures reinforce overall meaning	short words, words with similar visual patterns	short selections with few characters, one to two lines of text per page, clear and consistent type size and typeface	focus on consonants, rhyming patterns, phonograms, and phonetically regular words; greater use of high frequency words
Developing/Fluent Leveled Readers Grade 1: Level C Grade 2: 31B–60B Grade 3: 61A–90A	mix of speech and language patterns, some sentence variety	some text support to reinforce meaning, moderate picture-to-text match	story-like but short episodes, stories become more complex with several characters	more lines of text per page, consistent arrangement of text on page	focus on short vowels, long vowels, consonant blends, and digraphs

Scott Foresman Leveling System

Stage	Language Structure	Illustrations (Art and Photos)	Vocabulary, Concepts, Content, and Genre	Text Format and Features (Book Length, Size, and Layout)	Phonics and Word Study
Fluent Leveled Readers Grade 2: Level C Grade 3: 61B–90B Grade 4: 91A–120A	greater variety in sentence structure, some examples of compound sentences	illustrations reinforce overall meaning, conveys setting and atmosphere	more story-like with varied events, several characters, some specialized vocabulary, increase in content-area words, photos add support for nonfiction selections	longer selections with varied genres and literary styles, increase in nonfiction selections	focus on inflected endings, compound words, plurals, r-controlled vowels, and long and short vowels
Fluent/Proficient Leveled Readers Grade 3: Level C Grade 4: 91B–120B Grade 5: 121A–150A	written language forms and literary language predominate, greater variety in sentence structure, many more compound sentences	few illustrations to reinforce overall meaning, conveys setting and atmosphere	more specialized topics and vocabulary, increase in number of vocabulary words, photos add support for nonfiction selections	longer selections with varied genres and literary styles, increase in nonfiction selections	emphasis is on multisyllabic words
Proficient Leveled Readers Grade 4: Level C Grade 5: 121B–150B Grade 6: 151A–180A	well-developed events, more examples of literary language, greater variety in sentence structure, many compound sentences	varied styles to support overall meaning; conveys setting, atmosphere, and/or mood; partial pages with illustrations	more specialized topics and vocabulary, increase in number of vocabulary words	smaller type size fits full page, longer selections with varied genres and literary styles, increase in nonfiction selections	many examples of multisyllabic words
Proficient Leveled Readers Grade 5: Level C Grade 6: 151B–180B Grade 6: Level C	well-developed events, more examples of literary language, greater variety in sentence structure, many compound sentences, more sophisticated language structures	partial pages with illustrations, minimum picture support	increase in number of vocabulary words, challenging vocabulary incorporated	smaller type size fills full page; complex stories that describe setting, characters, problem(s), and resolution(s) in more detail	many examples of multisyllabic words

Observation Checklist

Student's Name _____ **Date** _____

Behaviors Observed	Always (Proficient)	Usually (Fluent)	Sometimes (Developing)	Rarely (Novice)

Reading Strategies and Skills

Behaviors Observed	Always (Proficient)	Usually (Fluent)	Sometimes (Developing)	Rarely (Novice)
Uses prior knowledge and preview to understand what book is about				
Makes predictions and checks them while reading				
Uses context clues to figure out meanings of new words				
Uses phonics and syllabication to decode words				
Self-corrects while reading				
Reads at an appropriate reading rate				
Reads with appropriate intonation and stress				
Uses fix-up strategies				
Identifies story elements: character, setting, plot structure, theme				
Summarizes plot or main ideas accurately				
Uses target comprehension skill to understand the text better				
Responds thoughtfully about the text				

Reading Behaviors and Attitudes

Behaviors Observed	Always (Proficient)	Usually (Fluent)	Sometimes (Developing)	Rarely (Novice)
Enjoys listening to stories				
Chooses reading as a free-time activity				
Reads with sustained interest and attention				
Participates in discussion about books				

General Comments

Taking a Running Record

A running record is an assessment of a student's oral reading accuracy and oral reading fluency. Reading accuracy is based on the number of words read correctly. Reading fluency is based on the reading rate (the number of words read per minute) and the degree to which the student reads with a "natural flow."

How to Measure Reading Accuracy

1. Choose a grade-level text of about 80 to 120 words that is unfamiliar to the student.

2. Make a copy of the text for yourself. Make a copy for the student or have the student read aloud from a book.

3. Give the student the text and have the student read aloud. (You may wish to tape-record the student's reading for later evaluation.)

4. On your copy of the text, mark any miscues or errors the student makes while reading. See the running record sample on page 9, which shows how to identify and mark miscues.

5. Count the total number of words in the text and the total number of errors made by the student. Note: If a student makes the same error more than once, such as mispronouncing the same word multiple times, count it as one error. Self-corrections do not count as actual errors. Use the following formula to calculate the percentage score, or accuracy rate:

$$\frac{\text{Total Number of Words} - \text{Total Number of Errors}}{\text{Total Number of Words}} \times 100 = \text{percentage score}$$

Interpreting the Results

- A student who reads **98–100%** of the words correctly is reading at an **independent level** and may need more challenging texts.

- A student who reads **91–97%** of the words correctly is reading at an **instructional level** and will likely benefit from guided instruction.

- A student who reads **90% or less** of the words correctly is reading at a **frustrational level** and may benefit most from targeted instruction with lower-level texts and intervention.

See the Scott Foresman Leveling System on pages 154 and 155 to help you select materials that are appropriate for the student's reading level.

How to Measure Reading Rate

1. Follow Steps 1–3 above.

2. Note the exact times when the student begins and finishes reading.

3. Use the following formula to calculate the number of words per minute (wpm), or reading rate:

$$\frac{\text{Total Number of Words Read}}{\text{Total Number of Seconds}} \times 60 = \text{words per minute}$$

Interpreting the Results

An appropriate rate is roughly equal to the student's age × 10, plus or minus 10. For example, a 9-year-old student should be reading 80–100 words per minute.

Anecdotal Record

Teacher _____

Date Student	Date Student

Student Self-Assessment

Student's Name _____ **Date** _____

Leveled Reader Title and Activity _____

Things I Did Well	Things I Need to Work On
_____	_____
_____	_____
_____	_____
_____	_____
_____	_____
_____	_____
_____	_____
_____	_____
How I Will Work on Them	**My Goals for the Future**
_____	_____
_____	_____
_____	_____
_____	_____
_____	_____
_____	_____
_____	_____
_____	_____

 Don't forget to share your self-assessment with your family! Talk about what you've read and done in class. Think of other ways you can practice your reading skills at home with your family.

Progress Report

Student's Name _____

At the top of the chart, record the book title, the accuracy rate, and the reading rate at which the student reads the Leveling System. See page 157 for taking a running record to calculate accuracy and reading rates. At the bottom of the chart, record the date you took the running record. In the middle of the chart, write *F, I, ID* across from the appropriate stage to indicate whether the student is reading at a frustrational level (below 90% accuracy), an instructional level (91–97% accuracy), or an independent level (98–100% accuracy). See the Scott Foresman Leveling System on pages 154–155 to find the stage at which the Leveled Reader is leveled.

Book Title, Accuracy Rate, Reading Rate												
S T A G E	Proficient											
	Fluent/Proficient											
	Fluent											
	Developing/Fluent											
	Novice/Developing											
	Early/Novice											
	Beginning											
Date												